LEVERAGE FACTORY

1473 NW Lewis St.
Bend, OR 97701

Be a Writer

YOUR GUIDE TO THE WRITING LIFE!

Proven Tips and Powerful Techniques to Help Young Writers Get Started

LEVERAGE FACTORY

1473 NW Lewis St.
Bend, OR 97701

STEVE PEHA
MARGOT CARMICHAEL LESTER

www.leveragefactory.com

Proven Tips and Powerful Techniques to Help Young Writers Get Started

Be a Writer

YOUR GUIDE TO THE WRITING LIFE

STEVE PEHA | MARGOT CARMICHAEL LESTER

www.beawriter.US

check it out!

Be a Writer—Your Guide to the Writing Life

Published by	The Leverage Factory, Inc.
Authors	Steve Peha & Margot Carmichael Lester
Development	The Word Factory
Copy	Pen Ultimate
Layout	Anny B. Thompson
Design	Pete Minnelli & Anny B. Thompson

Printed in the United States of America

Published by:

The Leverage Factory, Inc.
1473 NW Lewis St.
Bend, OR 97701

www.leveragefactory.com
www.beawriter.US

10 9 8 7 6 5 4 3 2 1

DEDICATION

To my mother, Donna Peha, my first teacher, and the one who taught me everything I know that really matters about how to help kids succeed.

To my father, Marc Peha, who passed away during the writing of this book. He was an enthusiastic storyteller always eager to find a new audience.

ABOUT THE AUTHORS

Steve Peha

 Steve Peha is a leading voice on reading, writing, and education reform. As the founder of Teaching That Makes Sense, Inc. (TTMS), he has developed strategies that help teachers deliver more effective instruction and help kids improve their literacy skills.

TTMS provides education consulting, teacher training, and classroom modeling to school districts in the U.S. and Canada using the Reader's and Writer's Workshop method. In his materials, workshops, and books, Steve combines the best of classroom practice with a real-world, results-oriented perspective that makes teaching more practical for teachers and learning more meaningful kids.

Since founding TTMS in 1995, Steve has delivered hundreds of workshops for teachers, administrators, and parents. He has also addressed school boards, PTAs, and other organizations to discuss current challenges in education reform.

A trusted source for education journalists, he is widely quoted in the media discussing everything from teacher pay and high-stakes testing to the Achievement Gap and No Child Left Behind. His comments and opinion pieces have appeared in USA Today, The Christian Science Monitor, The Atlanta Journal-Constitution, The Miami Herald, The Austin American-Statesman, and The Milwaukee Journal-Sentinel, as well as in School Reform News and District Administration magazines.

In 2001, Steve was asked by The Seattle Times to write *The Effective Learning Series*, a bi-weekly column on best practice teaching that won the Innovators in Education Award from the Newspaper Association of America. Over the years, he has contributed more than 200 columns to this program, most recently an 18-part series on life skills for high school students.

Steve holds a BA in English from Boston University. He lives in Charrboro, North Carolina, with his wife, Margot Carmichael Lester, and their dog, Ursa.

For more information on Steve, visit the Teaching That Makes Sense website at www.ttms.org.

.

Margot Carmichael Lester

Margot Carmichael Lester stays on top of two careers, plying her trade as a professional writer and also as a business consultant.

Margot's writing appears regularly in magazines and newspapers as well as on the web. Her business journalism has been featured in Money Magazine, Multifamily Executive Magazine, The Los Angeles Business Journal, The Los Angeles Downtown News, The Triangle Business Journal and the Raleigh (N.C.) News & Observer. She is the author of *The Real Life Guide to Life After College* and *The Real Life Guide to Starting Your Career*. Her career advice appears monthly on Monster.com and in newspaper and magazine stories nationally.

Margot is also a love advice columnist, writing weekly for Match.com and MSN. In this capacity, she is frequently quoted as a relationship expert in publications around the country and on local, regional, and internet radio stations.

Prior to founding The Word Factory, her writing and consulting business, Margot served as director of marketing for the nationally-ranked Kenan-Flagler Business School at the University of North Carolina at Chapel Hill.

Margot began her writing career in high school as the school page columnist for her hometown paper, The Chapel Hill (N.C.) News.

Margot holds a BA in Journalism from The University of North Carolina at Chapel Hill. She lives in Carrboro, North Carolina, with her husband, Steve Peha, and their dog, Ursa.

For more information on Margot, visit her website at www.margotlester.com.

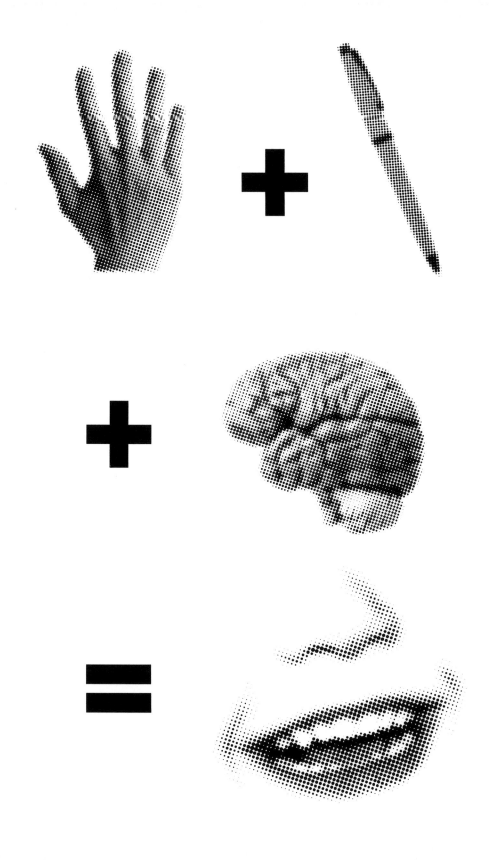

TABLE OF CONTENTS

LEVERAGE FACTORY

1473 NW Lewis St.
Bend, OR 97701

CHAPTER ONE: *Be a Writer*

CHAPTER TWO: *Be a Pre-Writer*

CHAPTER THREE: *Be a Drafter*

CHAPTER FOUR: *Be a Reviser*

CHAPTER FIVE: *Be an Editor*

CHAPTER SIX: *Be a Publisher*

CHAPTER SEVEN: *Be a Memoir Writer*

CHAPTER EIGHT: *Be an Essay Writer*

CHAPTER NINE: *Be an Editorial Writer*

CHAPTER TEN: *Be a Fiction Writer*

CHAPTER ELEVEN: *Be a Book Reviewer*

ACTIVITY INDEX

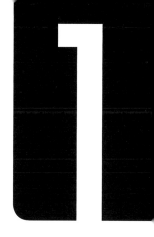

CHAPTER ONE

Be a Writer

TEN THINGS YOU NEED TO KNOW
EVEN IF YOU DON'T READ THIS CHAPTER

1 Writing is a meaningful and important activity that will change your life and the lives of the people who read your work.

2 Being a writer isn't necessarily fun, at least not all the time, but it's an important thing to do that makes a difference in the world.

3 Being a writer isn't about skill or achievement or getting an "A" in Language Arts; it's about thinking you're a writer and just doing it.

4 The best ideas for writing come from your own life experience.

5 Writers find topics everywhere, even in normal everyday experiences most of us never think about.

6 You can come up with many ideas for writing just by making a list of the typical things you do almost every day.

7 You can also come up with great topics by making a list of the unusual things that have happened to you in your life.

8 Your life is more interesting than you think; let your reader be the judge of what a good idea is and isn't.

9 When you get in the habit of thinking about ideas for writing, new ones will hit you out of the blue, and you'll know instantly that you have to write about them.

10 You know you've got a great topic when it's something you have strong feelings about and something you can talk about in great detail.

I HATE WRITING

"I hate writing. But I love having written."

This famous quote by Dorothy Parker perfectly captures the way I feel about writing. I hate it. I really do. There are a million things I'd rather do than write. For example, here are seven right off the top of my head:

SEVEN THINGS I'D RATHER DO THAN WRITE

1. Watch Star Trek re-runs
2. Play music
3. Take a nap
4. Read
5. Eat M&Ms
6. Hang out with friends
7. Surf the web

Don't think that coming up with this list was hard, or that it took me a long time. It wasn't and it didn't. Thinking of things I wish I were doing instead of writing is one of the most natural things I do. In fact, the third item, "Take a nap", is what I wish I were doing right now.

And yet I call myself a writer. I even write books. Ah, sweet mystery of life!

BECAUSE IT'S THERE

If you ask a man why he climbs a mountain, he will say, "Because it's there." I heard this many times when I was a kid and each time I heard it I thought it was stupid. I had vegetables on my dinner plate and I didn't eat them just because they were there. I had toys all over the floor of my room and I didn't pick them up just because they were there. As a kid, the only reason I did anything was because it was fun or because my mom told me I had to. I didn't do anything just because it was there. But as an adult, I write even though I really don't like it much, and I think I now understand the mountain climbing thing, too.

At the ripe old age of forty-two, my head is filled with ideas—the accumulation of a life spent thinking. But just thinking about things no longer works for me. I have to get these ideas out of my head and into the world, where other people can read them. You see, what really makes me write is the idea of my ideas becoming your ideas, and your life getting a little better as a result.

Your head is filled with ideas, too; everybody's is. Even if you're a lot younger than I am, and even if you don't care about climbing mountains, your ideas deserve to be written down and shared with others. Trust me on this. If there's one thing I know after twenty years of helping people learn to write, it's that everyone—every single person regardless of age, ability, or background—has something important to say.

I hope this book helps you find it.

WHY PEOPLE WRITE, REALLY

If you've been going to school longer than a day and a half, you've probably heard a teacher or two tell you about the purposes of writing. We write to tell stories. We write to inform. We write to persuade. We write to entertain. These are the reasons people write.

Not exactly.

This is just something we're taught in school, something that doesn't match up very well with how writers in the real world think about their work. Many things in school are like this. Especially things about writing.

The truth is that people write because they want you to think something, or because they want you to do something. Sometimes they even want both.

Take this book, for example.

After you read it, I want you to think that writing is a meaningful and important activity, something that will enrich your life and the lives of the people who read your work, even if the activity itself isn't always fun or easy. What I want you to do is start writing.

I'm not writing to tell you stories (though I may sneak in a few). I'm not writing to make you more informed (though there is information here). I'm not writing to persuade you of anything (though I think you'll find me credible). And finally, while I hope you find something entertaining in these pages, I'm not sitting here wearing out my keyboard just to show you a good time. If you're looking for entertainment, try skateboarding or go play with your Xbox. Writing is serious business.

And this, of course, is the real reason I think writers write: it makes us feel like serious people. It makes us feel important, as though what we say really matters because we put it down somewhere. We let it out into the world; a few people read it; a few of those people actually like it; and maybe someone believes it and it changes their life.

How about that for a purpose? Writers write to change people's lives. That *is* serious business. So I guess we'd better get to it.

ACTIVITY: WHY DO YOU WRITE?

If you're reading this book, you've either done some writing or you're about to. So why do you write? I've told you some reasons why I think writers write. Now think about your own. Most kids I talk to say they write because it's fun. But I often wonder if they have other more important reasons. Knowing why you write will help you write better. How? As you'll see in the next chapter, writing isn't always fun. When it isn't, we need other reasons to keep doing it.

WHY SOME PEOPLE ARE WRITERS AND OTHERS AREN'T

Whether or not you're a writer depends on which state you live in—state of mind, that is.

Our society believes that only some people are writers. What makes a person deserving of the title is talent or commercial success. Basically, if you write really well, or if you've made a lot of money writing, you get to call yourself a writer.

This is hogwash.

Where do we start learning things like this? Probably in school. Sometimes, school is a place where we learn that we can't be something (like a writer) because we can't do something (like pass a test or get an "A") because we don't have something else (like proper study habits or strong discipline). For example, if you get straight A's in Language Arts and you pass your state's writing test, you might be inclined to think of yourself as a writer. If you don't, you probably won't. If you go to college, and major in Creative Writing, you might think of yourself as a writer. If you don't, you probably won't.

Fortunately, school is but a small part of life and most of us eventually outgrow it. In reality, just about everyone is a writer. We live in the Information Age, and most of that information is written down somewhere by someone. Writing is a fact of modern life and being a writer is a fact of modern living.

EXAMPLE:

My mother-in-law is eighty years old. She left the workforce years ago. Other than taking care of herself and coming by our house to feed our dog, get our mail, and watch her favorite shows on cable when my wife and I are away, she doesn't have too many responsibilities. But she writes all the time. She sends several e-mails a day to friends and family. She keeps up with the people in her movie group. She probably writes a few thousand words a week. And when her computer is down, she tells us she feels cut off from the world because she can't write to people or read what they've written to her.

GOT WRITING?

If you put pencil or pen to paper, you're a writer. If you write e-mails or send instant messages, you're a writer. If u cn rd ths you're at least sending text messages on cell phones, and even though most people don't think of that as writing, it probably is. Heck, if you're reading this book, you can consider yourself a writer right now.

Lots of people ask my wife, who writes about 200 stories a year, primarily for magazines and websites, how they can be writers like she is. "Start writing!" she tells them. But instead of taking her advice, most simply want to take classes. They think that in order to be a writer they have to go to school. Nothing could be farther from the truth. In fact, the longer most of us go to school, the less likely it is that we will ever become writers.

Unless we're in a special program, or we're lucky enough to have a special teacher, the writing we do in school is often very different from the writing writers do in real life. In real life, writers don't spend much time writing book reports, character sketches, test answers, compare-contrast papers, literary analyses, and five-paragraph essays. School has its own unique set of writing rules and rituals, many of which never come up again after we graduate. Writing in school is sort of like practicing a sport but never getting to play a real game.

IT'S ALL IN YOUR HEAD

Writing is a state of mind that becomes a state of being: I think I'm a writer, therefore I write. But if you don't think you're a writer, you won't be one. That's just the way it is.

I look at it this way: Why *not* be a writer? What have you got to lose? It doesn't cost anything. And it's not like you need new clothes, a fancy haircut, or a secret decoder ring from a box of your favorite breakfast cereal. Why don't you just decide to start right now? Let the words fall where they may!

Miss Margot says

The only thing I ever found in my cereal that had anything to do with writing was a cool invisible pen set I got in a box of Quisp. I've thought of myself as a writer since I was six when I wrote a play. Looking back now, it was a very bad play. But I wrote it. And even though it wasn't very good, I knew from then on that I was a writer.

OKAY, WHERE DO I START?

Every piece of writing starts with an idea. But where do ideas start?

I took a class once on how to write music. It's not the same as writing stories, but it's pretty close. On the first day, the professor walked in, sat down at the piano, and said, "Where do ideas come from?" Then he played his piano for a while and told us stories of what it was like to be a pilot in World War II and have your plane shot down in enemy territory. His piano playing was kind of strange—his hands just drifted here and there over the keys—but his stories were spellbinding.

The next day he came in, sat down at the piano, started noodling around on the ivories again, and told more war stories. On the third day, he did the same thing. Every so often he'd punctuate a story with the now familiar refrain, "Where do ideas come from?"

This was how the class went. Four weeks of random piano playing, an endless supply of interesting war stories, and one perplexing question. Somehow, I got through the class even though I can't remember actually writing anything or even attempting to write anything. I guess I never figured out where ideas came from.

A few years later I started teaching my own writing classes.

Of course, I had the same challenge with my students that my music professor had with his: helping them come up with good ideas. Fortunately for my students, I didn't have a piano in the room or any war stories to tell, so I just told them what I realized my professor had been trying to tell me: ideas come from life experience.

TIP:

Perhaps the oldest and best piece of advice one writer can pass along to another is this: Write what you know. And what do you know better than your own life? After all, you've lived it as long as you've been alive. Many things have happened to you—things other people want to know about. Don't believe me? Read on and see what happens.

ACTIVITY: WHERE DID THAT IDEA COME FROM?

Have you ever wondered where the writers you read get ideas for their stories? You read novels all the time in school and every one of them was written by someone who had to come up with the idea first. The Internet is a great source of information about your favorite authors and how they got ideas for their books. Almost every book ever written has its own web page filled with information about it. To find websites for your book, go to your favorite search engine and type in the title inside quotation marks like this: "Be a Writer." The quotation marks are important, so don't forget them.

START WITH LITTLE THINGS

Every day we do hundreds of little things, so many that we really aren't aware of what they are. These little things take up a great deal of our time. They're also great opportunities for writing. Because we do these things so often, we know them very well. And because we know them very well, we probably have a lot to say about them.

Take right now, for example.

Right now, I'm waiting. I have a meeting with someone and I showed up early. This happens all the time. But somehow I never get used to it. I'm not a good waiter, never have been.

I spend a fair amount of my time waiting. I think we all do. As a kid, I didn't realize this. Like many kids, I was impatient. I couldn't just sit and wait for things; I always had to be doing something. As an adult, however, I'm less inclined toward being active all the time, and I like to think I can wait patiently the way other grown-ups do.

But I can't.

At times like these, I realize I'm just a little kid in a big body. I'm just as fidgety, just as restless as I was when I was young. I may not need to run around and yell and scream like I used to, but I do need to be engaged mentally, if nothing else.

So I make up games.

I solve math problems. I make lists. I think back through the book I'm reading (or, if I have the book with me, I read it). I think of songs I know, or make up new ones. I try to remember things I was supposed to do but have surely forgotten by now, and I plan to do them after I'm done doing the thing I'm waiting to do. Sometimes I just watch myself breathe (it's harder than you think and an interesting skill to master).

I've often thought that since I spend so much time waiting I might use these many minutes to develop a useful skill or somehow become a better person. Perhaps I could learn a language or memorize inspiring quotations by famous people.

But that would take too long. And I'm not a good waiter, never have been.

THAT'S WHAT WRITERS DO

How about that? I just wrote a piece. I think I'll call it "Waiting Games." I'm not sure it's a very good piece, but that's not the point. The point is that I wrote it. Because that's what writers do.

Right before your very eyes, I wrote a piece. Actually, I wrote it while I was waiting. Out of something that happens to me almost every day, an idea sprang forth, and I decided to write about it. Because that's what writers do.

It wasn't much of an idea, just a little one based on a little thing in my life. But I took some time to explore it and discovered, as I have so many times, that these little things can be the stuff of great writing. Because that's what writers do.

At this point in my life as a writer, I know I can take any moment of my day, pry it open just a bit, and look inside for a good idea. Sure enough, there are dozens of these "writeable moments" available to me. Finding them is actually pretty easy. Of course, then I have to decide which ones are worth writing about and motivate myself to write about them. Because that's what writers do.

Then there's the question of *how* to write about these things. Admit-tedly, topics as mundane as waiting, folding laundry, feeding the dog, or opening the refrigerator and realizing that we're out of milk don't automatically suggest a riveting storyline. To come up with something worth writing about, I have to look at it differently; I have to come up with an unusual way of talking about the usual. Because that's what writers do.

And then I have to write. This is the hard part. Anyone can think of an idea. But it takes a writer to write it down. Because that's what writers do.

Sometimes just a single line will come to me like, "Could there be anything more frustrating, more downright depressingly disappoint-ing, than opening the refrigerator door and discovering there's no milk just after you've poured yourself a potentially delicious bowl of your favorite cereal?" Sometimes, when I'm writing about the little things, I try to make them into big things. Because that's what writers do.

TIP:

Making mountains out of mole-hills is, in fact, a perfectly good way to make the less interesting more interesting. When the topic is small, we can write big. By contrast, when we're onto a big topic, we work hard in the other direc-tion, trying to say things simply, in a smaller way that doesn't crowd out the story itself. Because that's what writers do.

Ultimately, being a writer isn't about how good you are or how much money you make. It's about doing the things writers do. Mostly what writers do is look for ideas, look for the right words to express them, and then look for a piece of paper and something to write with. If you can do these three things, you can be a writer, too.

Miss Margot says

My friends are always talking to me about stuff they care about. They joke about how at some point, I'll write about it. That's because they know I'm always looking for ideas. I bet if you listened with a writer's ear to the things people say to you, you'd find a bunch of ideas, too.

BE A WRITER LIKE REBECCA ROBERTS

Rebecca Roberts writes radio features, TV stories, newspaper articles, and book reviews. Her work credits include reporting technology stories for "The World," a co-production of PRI, the BBC and WGBH Boston; guest hosting "Weekend America" from American Public Media; and hosting the Emmy-nominated public television series "Springboard" on PBS. Her work has been featured on public radio programs such as "Morning Edition," "All Things Considered" and "Studio 360." She was also the founding producer of the nationally distributed weekly public radio program "Beyond Computers." She was recently hired to host a new radio program called "The Intersection" for WETA in Washington D.C.

Q WHAT KIND OF WRITER ARE YOU?

A I'm strictly a non-fiction news writer. I admire the heck out of people who can develop characters and dialog and plot lines, but I ain't one of 'em.

I tend to write in my head. I play around with structure and word choice while I'm driving, or checking e-mail, or falling asleep at night, or taking a shower. By the time I actually sit down at the keyboard, it's really just typing—the story is largely written already. I rarely revise more than once, unless an editor makes me.

Q WHY DO YOU WRITE?

A I love to tell stories, but I tell stories that are true, new, strange, and complicated. I write to bring the story clarity and power. I write to give a story an audience. I write because the English language is a rich, crazy, illogical mishmash that can become a thing of beauty in the right hands. My hands aren't always the right ones, but I can't stop trying.

Q

WHAT MADE YOU WANT TO BE A WRITER?

If you love books, and love stories, and love words, I think you can't help but try to write. I never had the imagination or talent to write fiction, so I chose news. But don't think news isn't creative—especially radio, where you need to create the pictures in the listeners' minds.

Q

WHAT ADVICE WOULD YOU GIVE TO A FELLOW WRITER WHO WAS JUST STARTING OUT?

Learn the basics first. I know it sounds boring, but even the best story ever told can be crippled by lousy grammar, lazy spelling, or awkward word choice. It's like a cubist painter mastering classical figure drawing. Once you've got a good handle on grammar and usage, you can get as edgy and innovative as you want, but you have to know what you're doing first.

Read your writing out loud. If it feels wrong in your mouth, it's not authentic.

Think about what you love about your favorite writers. Don't imitate them, but try to capture their strengths and add your own mark.

Write every day.

LOOKING FOR LITTLE THINGS

As I just said, being a writer involves looking for ideas, looking for words, and looking for paper and something to write with. It's a lot of looking. But it's a lot of doing, too, and I've been doing my bit for the past several pages. So now it's your turn. Don't worry, though; I'll be working right along with you every step of the way.

MAKING LISTS

Just about every topic selection strategy I know involves making lists of one kind or another. So that's what we're going to do. We'll start with a list of little things from our lives. I'm thinking about the typical things that happen to me almost every day or at least on a regular basis.

TYPICAL THINGS IN MY LIFE

- Reading

- Getting behind on my e-mail

- Struggling to get up in the morning

- Not playing music when I really want to

- Not exercising or watching what I eat

- Driving

- Waiting (for people, for airplanes, for everything!)

- Watching sports with my wife

- Going out to eat

- Trying to stop drinking so much Coca Cola (and remarking on the ridiculous proliferation of new Coke varieties)

- Traveling for work

- Eating dessert

- Taking airplane trips

- Fixing my computer when it breaks

- Talking to teachers about teaching

- Hanging out with our dog

- Going to the Dead Mule

- Watching bad TV when I should be doing something else

- Staying in hotels

This is always an interesting exercise for me. No matter how often I do it, I realize something new about myself. This time, I had a harder time making this list than I have in the past. I think it's because my life right now is kind of crazy. I'm traveling all over the country every month these days, working in schools. My life is anything but typical at the moment. But it still has typical elements, patterns of activity that occur for me on a regular basis.

ACTIVITY: MAKE YOUR OWN LIST OF LITTLE THINGS

Okay, I went first. Now you try it. Just start thinking of things you do on a regular basis. Start by looking for simple things that are part of your daily routine. For example, I came up with "Reading" which I do every night to fall asleep, "Getting behind on my e-mail", which happens to me every time I travel, and "Struggling to get up in the morning", which has been true for me most of my life.

Once you've put down some of your regularly scheduled daily and weekly activities, think about things you do often, even if they aren't on a regular schedule. For example, you and your family may not go out to eat dinner every Tuesday and Friday night, but you might do it once or twice a month. And while you might be reading this book in the middle of winter, you may remember that when spring comes around, you'll be going to baseball practice almost every day.

HOW MANY THINGS DO YOU HAVE TO HAVE?

Say you wrote down two things and then you got stuck. Well, two's better than none, I guess. And yet, this is not exactly the kind of output we were hoping for, is it? Often, when I teach this lesson in school, kids want to know how many ideas they're supposed to have. I tell them there is no right number. But I also tell them this:

- **Come up with as many topics as you can.** Many of the topics we choose to write about don't end up turning into good pieces. That's just the way it is. So it's nice if we can have a ready list of other ideas to turn to when the first one we pick doesn't work out.

- **Most folks get a dozen or so.** The record for most topics on a list during a fifteen-minute lesson in school is seventy-two by a fifth grader from Shawnee Mission, Kansas. Most of the time, people who do this come up with ten to twenty topics just like I did.

- **You only need a few good ones.** It isn't really about quantity; it's about quality. But since we don't know yet which topics will be better than others, we try to write down as many as we can at this point.

TIP:

If you're struggling to come up with ideas, try these strategies:

- **Get more specific.** You'll notice on my list that I wrote "Watch sports with my wife." I could get more topics out of that if I wrote down which sports we watch: NFL Football, college basketball (Go Heels!), and NASCAR. (I don't really understand NASCAR yet, but my wife says that's just because I haven't lived in the South long enough.)

- **Divide your life into categories.** To come up with more topics, think of your big list as being made up of other lists: typical things at home, typical things at school, typical things on the weekend, typical things you do with friends, and so on.

- **Write down a few things that don't seem to matter.** Everybody eats; everybody sleeps; everybody brushes their teeth (or at least they should). Put a bunch of these things down. Even if they don't turn out to be good topics for writing, the act of writing them down will give you some momentum, and that may make you think of something else.

- **Think of "not" things.** We all have things we think about doing regularly but don't do for various reasons. In my case, I listed "not exercising or watching what I eat" and "not playing music." What's typical for me is wishing that I was doing these things, and then ending up not doing them. Everyone has these "not" things, and sometimes they make great writing topics.

If you don't get a ton of topics right off the bat, don't worry about it. Put this exercise away. Maybe it's not a good one for you. Or maybe you just don't like it. If that's true, don't do it. Yep, that's right. Bag it. It's no big deal. I'm serious. This is not an assignment; those are for school.

There are things I hope you learn from me, even if you don't learn to write well enough to become rich and famous. One is how to manage your own writing process. There are as many different ways to write as there are writers writing. If something I suggest doesn't work for you, wait until I suggest something else, or figure out your own way and do that. Another thing I want you to learn is ownership. This is your writing, not mine. You're responsible for it. That means it's not only up to you to figure out how to do it; it's up to you to decide whether it's worth doing at all.

I'm sure there are tons of teachers, coaches, tutors, and parents out there who'll say your have to go it one and make yourself do everything somebody like me tells you to do; otherwise you won't learn. I feel differently. If some strategy I suggest isn't working, try the next one. Or just stop trying altogether and take a break.

TIP:

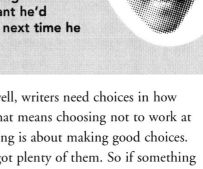

Taking a break can be a legitimate writing strategy. Many writers, including yours truly, have made a fine art of strategic break taking. In fact, it is said that the great Ernest Hemingway used to stop writing in the middle of something he was working on because that meant he'd know exactly how to get started the next time he sat down to work.

The point is that in order to write well, writers need choices in how they get their work done—even if that means choosing not to work at all. Like so many things in life, writing is about making good choices. And if you've got this book, you've got plenty of them. So if something in your writing isn't turning out the way you want it to, just turn the page.

Miss Margot says

You never know when a good idea will conk you on the head. And now that you're on the lookout for good ideas, do something to hold on to them. I keep a list of good ideas on my computer so I can jot them down whenever I trip over one. I also keep pads of paper in my car and on my bedside table so I can scribble down an idea before it gets away.

ACTIVITY: FIND A PLACE TO PUT YOUR WRITING

I just asked you to make a list of potential topics to write about. But where are you going to put that list when you're done? Many writers I know keep notebooks. Some notebooks are full-size, like the kind you have in school. But more often, writers keep tiny notebooks with them, sometimes in their back pocket. My best friend, Pete Andersen, keeps three notebooks: one for writing ideas about his kids, one for writing ideas that are not about his kids, and one just for lists (he loves making lists). You need **to** figure out where you're going to keep your writing. Of course, you'll probably keep most of it in your computer. But you should also have a paper place— a notepad, notebook, journal, napkin, or dollar bill—so you can jot down ideas at any time.

WHAT MAKES THIS WRITING GOOD?

Here's a piece about a typical part of life we can all relate to. It's a perfect example of how we can find good topics to write about in our everyday lives.

Chores!

Chores! Chores! Chores! Chores are boring! Scrubbing toilets, cleaning sinks, and washing bathtubs take up a lot of my time and are not fun at all.

Toilets! When you're scrubbing toilets make sure they're not stinky. I've scrubbed one before and I was lucky it didn't stink. I think toilets are one of the hardest things to scrub in the bathroom because it's hard to get up around the rim.

Sinks are one of the easiest things to clean in the bathroom because they have no rims and they are small. I cleaned one before and it was pretty easy.

Bathtubs, ever washed one? They're big, they're deep, and it's hard to get up around the sides. The bathtub is the hardest, I think, to wash in the bathroom.

➡

Chores are boring, especially making my bed. Cleaning my room is OK because I like organizing. Dusting is the worst: dust, set down, pick up, dust, set down. There are so many things to dust, and it's no fun.

Chores aren't the worst but they're definitely not the best!

What I love most about this piece is the voice. The writer's personality comes through loud and clear. It sounds like a real person who gets really frustrated with chores.. But there's more to like here than the author's tone.

Look at the sentences. She does a wonderful job of mixing short ones with long ones. She also uses sentences with many different structures. Read over the fourth and fifth paragraphs, for example. Almost every sentence is slightly different in how it is put together from the sentence that comes before or after. This kind of variety makes it fun to read the piece out loud.

Some of the details in the piece are very good, too. I especially like the part about dusting at the end. She could have just told us that dusting is repetitive. But instead she shows us what it's like with the descriptive sequence, "dust, set down, pick up, dust, set down." If you've ever done any dusting you know that's exactly how it feels.

As much as I love this piece and admire the writer who wrote it, I wish the ending was better. It's not that it's bad. It's just that it's not quite as good, in my opinion, as the rest of the piece. But this would be an easy thing to improve with one more revision.

LOOKING FOR BIG THINGS

You'd think that finding big things to write about would be easier than finding little things, if for no other reason than their size. Little things hide out in the mundane moments of everyday existence, but big things should be easy to spot.

And yet, they are not.

I can stand up in front of a group of 50 kids and say, "Anything unusual happen to anyone recently?" And not a single hand will go up. "Nothing unusual ever happens to us," someone will say. And then others will chime in, "Yeah, our lives are boring."

And yet, this is almost certainly untrue.

We humans have an odd way of looking at the things that happen to us in our lives. We tend to forget things we should easily remember and remember things we should easily forget. If something really unusual happened to me, you'd think I'd never forget it. But when pressed to come up with things that have happened in my life, I'm much more likely to recall brushing my teeth this morning than I am to remember the huge car accident I had five years ago.

And yet, I did just remember the huge car accident I had five years ago.

REMEMBERING BY REMEMBERING

This is exactly how remembering works. We start out by thinking we can't remember much of anything. Then we remember one thing that probably isn't something we wanted to remember. Then we remember something else, and maybe something else after that until finally, if we're lucky, we remember the thing we're really looking for.

Memory is *associative*, as the brain scientists tell us; everything we know is linked to something else. That means we need to make connections between things in order to retrieve memories. One of the best ways to make connections is with categories. So as I look for unusual things from my life that I think might make good topics for writing, I'm going to think of them in groups defined by certain kinds of unusual experiences.

TIP:

Here are several categories of unusual experiences that have worked well for me and for the students I have taught:

- **Accidents, Illnesses, and Injuries.** Hopefully these are unusual experiences in your life. They have been in mine. When I think about this category, I can remember that big car accident, breaking my finger before a big basketball game, falling down and hitting my head so badly I had to go to the emergency room, having a super-high fever for two weeks, and swallowing a pin when I was a little baby. I don't actually remember this last one, but my mom told me about it so many times I probably know enough to write about it.

- **Trips.** Just about everybody has taken a trip somewhere. Trips are great to write about because they present to us so many new and different things, and because we usually have very strong emotions about them. I take trips all the time for work, so I'm going to list some of the personal trips I've taken. I went to Mexico when I was in high school. I took a trip to New Orleans to get married and a trip to Paris for my honeymoon. My wife and I drove across the country when we moved to North Carolina. Any of these would probably make a good story.

- **Fame.** Have you ever met a famous person, or grown up with someone who became famous? (If you are a famous person, this category will be easy for you.) Fame always excites us and captures our attention, so it's a great thing to write about. I've met a few famous people: the magician David Copperfield, the billionaire Bill Gates, and pop star Barry Manilow. (I know. You've probably never heard of Barry Manilow. Ask your parents.) I also went to school with a guy named Anthony Ray who eventually became the rapper Sir Mix-A-Lot. And (I always save this one for last) in seventh grade Social Studies class I sat right next to—fanfare, please—none other than Duff McKagan, the bass player for the rock group Guns N' Roses.

- **Fortune.** Money makes the world go 'round. But it also makes for some interesting stories. Ever won some? Lost some? Earned some? Found some? Been given some? Spent some? I can still remember the time the old man down at the corner store didn't give me back the right change from my candy. I ran all the way home crying to my mother. As it turns out, he did this to a lot of little kids in our neighborhood, so we all had to learn to do our money math carefully. Now that's a great story. Other high-dollar highlights from my life include the time I lost a quarter on the 1971 Super Bowl (I was only seven and twenty-five cents was a lot of money back then), the time I won the Daily Double at Longacres racetrack (I didn't actually win it because I placed the bet incorrectly), and the sports-betting operation I ran in the library during my junior year of high school. (Seems like gambling plays quite a role in my life, doesn't it? Do you think I might have a problem? Nah. Don't believe me? I can quit any time I want. Wanna bet?)

- **Victory and Defeat.** Have you ever won anything or lost anything (other than money) that was really important to you? Most of us have stories about epic wins and losses in our lives. I still remember winning my first chess tournament. I also remember losing the biggest fish I ever hooked. Strangely, I don't seem to have much memory, or even any strong feelings, about the time my parents told me they were getting divorced. So even though that qualifies as a big loss in my life, it might not be a good writing topic for me.

- **Getting in Trouble.** This is one of my favorite categories when I run writing workshops for kids and adults. We've all done things we shouldn't have and gotten in trouble. (Yes, even you.) I remember the time I broke a window playing baseball in the house. I remember staying too late at a party and lying to my mom about it. I remember acting up in class once when we had a substitute and doing everything I could to get sent to the office.

- **Happy Times, Sad Times, Scary Times, Exciting Times, Special Times.** There was a TV commercial back when I was a kid (I think it was for cameras or film) that was all about remembering "the times of your life." Writing about something is sort of like taking a picture of it; the pictures most of us like to take are ones that go with our strongest feelings. Sometimes, looking back at your life through these emotional categories can help you come up with great ideas.

Now that I'm armed with categories and a few examples for each, I'm ready to make my big list of big things to write about. These are the unusual experiences, things that don't happen to me every day, or even every month or every year. These are things that may have happened to me only once in my life. That's part of what makes them worth writing about.

UNUSUAL THINGS IN MY LIFE

- My big car accident
- Breaking my finger before a big basketball game
- Falling down and hitting my head so badly that I had to go to the emergency room
- Meeting my wife for the first time at Burbank airport
- Having a super-high fever for two weeks
- The time when I was a little baby and I swallowed a pin
- My trip to Mexico when I was in high school
- The time my wife and I drove across the country to move to North Carolina

- My trip to New Orleans when we got married

- My honeymoon in Paris

- Meeting magician David Copperfield

- The three times I've met Bill Gates

- Meeting Barry Manilow

- Spending 6th grade with future rapper Sir Mix-A-Lot

- Sitting next to Duff McKagan, the bass player for Guns N' Roses, in 7th grade Social Studies

- The time the old man down at the corner store didn't give me the right change for my candy

- The time I lost a quarter at the 1971 Super Bowl

- The time I won the Daily Double at Longacres racetrack

- The sports-betting operation I ran in the library during my junior year of high school

- Winning my first chess tournament

- Losing the biggest fish I ever hooked

- The time I broke a window playing baseball in the house

- The time I stayed too late at a party and lied to my mom about it

- The time I acted up in class when we had a substitute and did everything I could to get sent to the office

So there you have it: a long list of big things to write about.

ACTIVITY: MAKE YOUR OWN LIST OF UNUSUAL EXPERIENCES

Now you take a shot. Start thinking back through your life for unusual occurrences. Write down anything that comes to mind. If you get stuck, review the categories I used, or feel free to make up some of your own. Just as before, don't get down if you can't come up with a bunch of ideas. Sometimes, when you're a writer, that's just the way it is.

Miss Margot says

Sometimes editors ask me to send them a list of stories I'd like to write. Sometimes it's easy and I come up with tons of them. Other times it's harder and I wonder if I'll ever have a good idea again. That's when I do stuff totally unrelated to writing. I read the paper, pick up a magazine, call a friend, or even go for a walk. For some reason only big-brained scientists understand, by *not* thinking about story ideas, I get a million story ideas.

ACTIVITY: OPPOSITES ATTRACT

Another neat way of coming up with topics involves making two lists at the same time. When I teach this to kids in school we call it the "Topic T-Chart" strategy. The strategy works by having you write up two lists side by side based on categories that are exact opposites. Here are the paired lists I use most frequently:

- **Like-Hate:** Things you like and things you hate.

- **Fun-Have To:** Things you do for fun and things you do because you have to.

- **Regret-Proud Of:** Things you regret and things you are proud of.

- **Change-Stay Same:** Things you want to change and things you want to stay the same.

Here's an example of a Topic T-Chart from a student I once worked with:

LIKE	HATE
Pizza	All vegetables
The Internet	Homework
Ice cream	Science
Music	Spelling tests
Reading	Getting dressed up
My cat	Cleaning my room
Harry Potter	Rainy days
Soccer	Being bored
Candy	Bowling

Considering two lists of opposites seems to help the writers I work with attract more topics to their lists. Sometimes a topic even ends up on both sides at the same time. When that happens, I highly recommend you write about it. A topic that ends up on both sides of a topic T-chart can be very powerful because you can explore two conflicting sets of feelings about it.

BRINGING YOUR LIFE TO LIFE

As I look back over my list of big things, I had two immediate reactions. First of all, it seems I've lived a more interesting life than I thought. Remember when I said that most of us think our lives are boring? I'm no different. My life doesn't feel special to me; it just feels like my life. But when I look at it with a writer's eye, it starts to look different, maybe a little more interesting. I'll bet your life does, too.

The second thing I noticed is that I never once thought of writing about any of these things... until now. Now, each of them supiour in seems like a possible piece. The simple act of thinking of them and writing them down has changed the way I feel about the ideas and about how I might be able to use things that have happened to me in my writing.

This is what I meant before about "being a writer". Under normal circumstances, I'm inclined to regard my life as a bunch of stuff. But when I think of myself as a writer, that stuff looks different. All of a sudden, it's not just stuff; it's inspiration.

And this is how being a writer changes your life. One minute you've got stuff; the next minute—BAM!—inspiration strikes. And it kind of feels that way, too. Stuff just hits you all of a sudden, like those lightning bolts in cartoons, but without all the smoke and screaming.

I know I'm getting into some weird philosophy here but stick with me for a second because what I'm about to tell you is really important— or at least it is to me.

For most mere mortals, every moment that passes just passes and that's it. Tuesday, September 27, 2005; 8:41PM and 17 seconds. Gone. Just like that. And there's nothing I can do to bring that moment back to life.

Unless I'm a writer.

If I'm a writer, I can write, "It was Tuesday, September 27, 2005. At precisely 8:41PM and 17 seconds, the index finger of my left hand struck the 'B' key on my keyboard as I began a section called 'Bringing Your Life to Life' in what would surely become the greatest book ever written about writing."

Arguably, some moments are not worth reviving, but others are. If you're a writer you can bring them back from oblivion just by putting pen to paper (or finger to keyboard in my case). Everything that has happened in the past, is happening now, or will happen in the future can inspire you to write.

I think that's pretty cool.

Being a writer brings your life to life. All that stuff that used to be just stuff has now been transformed. Your life is now filled with inspiration. Every moment that goes by is a potential idea. Watch out for lightning bolts!

Miss Margot says

Sometimes even ideas "not worth reviving" can be. In the South, where I come from, there's a rich tradition of storytelling. Almost every time someone tells a story, it gets better. One day I got stuck in a dressing room. It wasn't that exciting, but after about the tenth time I told the story, it was rip-roaring hilarious, with the police being called in and old ladies fainting. Now, I'm not saying you should lie, but sometimes when you're writing fiction, you can make even boring stuff seem more exciting.

WHAT'S A GOOD IDEA?

Two exercises, two lists, forty-four ideas, and several deep insights about living the writing life. How much more great work can a writer do in one day? I'm wiped out. Remember that nap I wanted to take way back on page 2? Now I feel like I deserve it.

Sometimes, as writers, we spend more time congratulating ourselves than we do actually writing. There's a reason for this: writing is hard. While it's true that I'm a writer simply by virtue of calling myself one and putting words on paper, most of us aspire to an even higher calling: we want to be good writers.

This is where writing gets hard.

It's true that I just came up with forty-four ideas, but are any of them any good? That is, if I can summon up the courage to write about one of these topics, will my writing actually appeal to my readers?

Not knowing who my readers are and not having even a sentence to give them, I realize I have no answer. But at least I have a question: What's a good idea?

Just having ideas is not enough. You have to have good ones and, even worse, you have to begin developing a kind of "writerly sixth sense" about which ideas are likely to be better than others. Your life will present you with many ideas, but you can only write about one at a time, so you have to learn to make the right choices.

TIPS FOR CHOOSING GOOD TOPICS

It's true what they say: you have to suffer for your art. But actually you don't have to suffer too much in this case because I've got a simple technique you can use to figure out whether an idea is worth writing about.

TIP:

To see how well an idea stacks up, ask yourself these questions:

1. **Do you have strong feelings about it?** How much a writer cares about a topic is probably the best predictor of success with the finished piece. If you care about your topic, you'll put more effort into writing about it, and this extra effort will lead to better work. Another neat thing that happens when you have strong feelings about a topic is that your voice gets better. I'm not talking about a cold remedy here. Voice, in writing, is the personal quality of a piece; it's how your unique personality comes through to shape the words in ways that make them different from anyone else's. It's also the aspect of your work that will be most interesting to the majority of your readers.

2. **Do you know a lot about it?** Writing is really two activities wrapped up into one. The first activity involves coming up with the ideas you plan to write about. The second involves expressing those ideas in ways that are interesting and understandable to your readers. The simple truth is, you can't do the second if you haven't done the first.

3. **Can you talk about it in great detail?** Details are the heart of any good piece of writing. Details are also what make your writing different from anyone else's. Part of knowing a lot about your topic is knowing the little things about it that your readers probably don't know.

ACTIVITY: CHECK YOUR IDEAS

For each idea you've come up with so far, give it a check mark if you have strong feelings about it. Give it another check mark if you know a lot about it. Give it a third check mark if you think you can talk about it in great detail. Topics with three check marks are probably your best bet for producing great pieces of writing.

TWO OUT OF THREE AIN'T BAD—OR IS IT?

Not every topic passes the "What's a Good Idea?" test. In fact, most don't. Why? Because you have to score high on all three criteria, two out of three usually isn't good enough.

But how can you know this much about a piece that isn't even written yet? Often you can't. Most of the time, we have to do at least a little bit of writing before we know whether or not a topic will work for us. Sometimes we don't even know then.

One of the hardest things about writing is all the not knowing. When we look at a blank page, we may not know what to write about. If we come up with a topic, we may not know what to write about it. If we come up with something to write, we may not know if it's good. And even if we write something good, we may not know whether anyone else will ever read it.

Writing is a double act of faith. You have to have faith in yourself because you have to believe you have something to say. But you also have to have faith in others because you have to believe they will be able to hear you. This is not an easy thing. Perhaps one of the reasons there are so few people in the world who call themselves writers is because there are so few people in the world who can sustain this kind of faith.

But you can.

THAT MOUNTAIN CLIMBING THING AGAIN

Remember what I said about climbing mountains all the way back on page 3? I said that if you asked a man why he climbs a mountain, he would say, "Because it's there."

Writing is no different.

Why search your life for an important topic to write about? Because it's there. Why struggle to remember an important detail? Because it's there. Why wrack your brain for the perfect word when probably any old word will get you by? Because it's there. The perfect word is there, just like the perfect topic or the perfect message. And if you're a writer, you have to write about it.

So if you're ready to climb the mountain, I'll be proud to be your guide. Turn the page and off we'll go.

CHAPTER TWO

Be a Pre-Writer

TEN THINGS YOU NEED TO KNOW
EVEN IF YOU DON'T READ THIS CHAPTER

1 The hardest thing about being a writer is sitting down and writing even when the page is blank and the words aren't coming to you.

2 Pre-writing is something writers do before they start writing. It makes writing easier by helping you develop things to write about.

3 Pre-writing isn't the only way to beat writer's block, but it's probably the best way.

4 Free writing is the most traditional and probably the most popular pre-writing strategy, but it doesn't often yield the best results because it lacks structure.

5 Despite the popularity of webbing and outlining techniques in school, professional writers rarely use them.

6 The best pre-writing strategies seem to be those that balance structure and freedom.

7 The Action-Feelings-Setting strategy is perfect for any single scene in a narrative.

8 Use the Transition-Action-Details strategy any time you're describing a sequence of events.

9 If you're working on something where a logical argument is important, the What-Why-How strategy can be a powerful pre-write.

10 You can use the Content-Purpose-Audience strategy as a pre-write for any type of writing.

I LOVE HAVING WRITTEN

I'm sitting at my computer, eager to get started. But I can't start. I'm absolutely serious. I woke up this morning intent on beginning this chapter. But now that I'm sitting here in front of my computer, I can't write a thing.

I've been looking blankly at an empty screen for about 15 minutes. In that time I've organized some papers on my desk, looked out the window a few times, answered an e-mail to my editor, cleaned my glasses, and turned on an extra light to cheer up my office on this dreary fall day.

Or maybe I'm the one who's dreary.

Three or four times now I've placed my fingers on the home row of my keyboard hoping, I guess, that they would start typing something on their own. They haven't. For the life of me, I can't remember how I was planning to start this chapter. And I suspect that even if I do remember, I won't like it anymore.

I don't feel good. It's about 11AM on a Saturday; I slept in late this morning, but all I can think of is going back to bed. I'm a little shivery (it's probably just nerves) but I think I may be getting a stomach-ache.

I'M NOT MAKING THIS UP

You're going to think I made this up as a way to start the chapter, but I didn't. This is how it is for me right now. I have an editor, a designer, and a publisher waiting for my work. I have a deadline to meet and right now, I'm not meeting it. This project is on a tight schedule; I need to have a good day.

When I get stuck like this, especially at the beginning of a chapter, I panic just a little. Even though I've been writing professionally for almost twenty years, a tiny part of my brain says, "I guess that's that. No more ideas. Your life as a writer is over."

This is nonsense, of course. But it's powerful nonsense and it has been working on me ever since I sat down to write this morning. There was a time in my life when being in this situation would have caused me to simply give up for the day. And on a certain level, there's really nothing wrong with that. But over the years, I've learned some tricks for dealing with this problem. And since this is what I had originally intended to talk to you about in this chapter, maybe what I'm feeling right now will help me find my focus.

Maybe.

THE HARDEST THING ABOUT BEING A WRITER

The hardest thing about being a writer is sitting down and writing. Being a writer is so much easier when your words are already there on the page in front of you and all you need to do is touch them up a bit or admire them. But before they can be touched up or admired, someone has to write them. And at the moment, I am that someone.

This is one of those times that I truly hate writing: when the page is empty and so am I. But this is also one of those times when being a writer is most important. If I didn't know I was a writer—if I wasn't 110% certain—moments like this would wipe me out. Instead, they are merely annoying.

Even though I'm having trouble starting the second chapter of this book, I know I'll be able to finish it and all the other chapters, too, because I can picture the finished book in my hands and I can see my name on the cover. I know, too, that I may face the problem I'm having now many times during the course of this project. It may slow me down but it won't stop me because even though I hate writing (especially at times like this), I absolutely love having written.

PRE-WRITING TO BE WRITING

There's nothing more intimidating than a blank page. The worst part is how silly most writers feel being intimidated by it. The page just sits there, staring at us, and we stare back, unable to do anything. There's so much blank space to fill, and so little inside us to fill it up with. It doesn't seem fair, and it's not. So every writer needs to bring something in to help level the playing field, something called *pre-writing*.

WHAT IS PRE-WRITING?

As its name implies, pre-writing is something you do before you start writing to make the process easier and the quality of your writing better. For example, we all do a little bit of thinking before we write—or at least we should. Pre-writing is a way to focus our thoughts and help us through the pain of writer's block.

Maybe we don't have a topic. Even if we do, we might not know exactly what we want to say about it. The fun of pre-writing is that it doesn't matter whether we know what we're doing or not. Pre-writing is a time we can use to experiment, to jot down ideas, to try new things without having to try very hard, to take a little time to gather our thoughts, and to choose a direction before we start drafting.

WHAT CAN I DO DURING PRE-WRITING?

You can do just about anything you want. You can draw. You can make notes. You can scribble random thoughts. Anything that will help you draft more effectively qualifies as pre-writing. I'll give you some special pre-writing strategies in the next few sections.

The great thing about pre-writing is that it doesn't really matter what you do, as long as it involves turning on your brain and thinking about your topic. Then, just write down whatever pops into your head. As you begin to put ideas on the page, you may start to see how you can organize them. Take your time. There's no rush. The time you spend pre-writing is time well spent.

WHY IS PRE-WRITING IMPORTANT?

If you play a sport or musical instrument, you know it's always a good idea to warm up before you start. That's what pre-writing is: a warm-up. It gets your mind loose and limber so that by the time you're ready to start drafting, you can push the pen around the page without straining your brain too much.

Maybe you've had this feeling in school: the teacher says it's time to write about something and you just sit there thinking, "I don't know what to write." You're just not warmed up. And everybody knows you can't play your best when you're not warmed up. So if you do a little pre-writing before you take the field, chances are your writing game will be much better for it.

EXAMPLE:

I got up this morning to write, but couldn't come up with anything to write about. So I used an old pre-writing trick: write about why you can't write. Not only did it help me get started, it also helped me come up with new material, some of which you're reading right now.

WHAT IF I DON'T WANT TO DO PRE-WRITING?

[Author's Note: Read this paragraph with a grumpy old man voice.] What do you mean you don't want to do pre-writing? Why, when I was in school, we weren't even *allowed* to do pre-writing! The teacher just told us to start drafting, and boy, was that a mess. We'd be writing away, not having any idea what we were doing, and then— BLAMMO! We'd all get writer's block. Pencils froze up mid-sentence. Sweat started streaming from our brows. The air became thick with the palpable anxiety of students who knew they were in for it. (I think some even had to go to the nurse.) All I can say is, you don't know how lucky you are to have someone like me telling you to do your pre-writing.

It's sort of like telling you to eat your vegetables, isn't it? Fat lot of good that does!

Truth is, I work with many writers, both kids and adults, who don't like pre-writing at all. They think it's a waste of time and they often get frustrated with me when I make them do it. They'd rather just start drafting. If that's how you feel, go right ahead and draft.

But every writer eventually reaches a point when the words won't come and the drafting won't go. Then we're faced with a choice: we can give up, or we can give in to the simple truth that when we don't know what to write, pre-writing is probably the best solution.

Miss Margot says

When I sit down to write, I'm always tempted to start drafting right away. Except, of course, I don't. You see, *everyone* pre-writes—even me. I just pre-write in my head instead of on paper. I let the idea bang around in my head for a while before I start writing, so the story starts taking shape before I ever begin typing at the computer.

FREEDOM TO WRITE

Ah, freedom! What red-blooded American writer doesn't appreciate the wide open spaces of a fresh page to write on and the freedom to write anything on it? That's right, anything at all. You don't have to write in sentences. Or even straight lines. Write upside down or backwards if that's what you feel like doing.

Perhaps the oldest, and in some sense, most sacred approach to pre-writing is called "free-writing." Within this venerable tradition, many variations exist. But the intent has always been the same: to make writers feel more comfortable and less inhibited as they search for new ideas.

FREE-WRITING

If you've been to school, or to a writer's workshop outside of school, you've probably had some experience with this. The concept is simple: just write. That's it. Put your pencil on the paper, or your fingers on the keyboard, and watch what happens. We're all nervous about writing. As a result, we tend to censor ourselves, blocking our best ideas because we're worried they might not be any good. Free-writing takes the edge off.

While the theory of free-writing makes sense, I don't use it very often in my own writing life. Occasionally it has helped me, as it did earlier in this chapter, but most of the time it hasn't been very useful.

EXAMPLE:

Here's a free-write I did just a minute ago on one of the topics from my lists. The topic I chose was "eating dessert."

I love eating dessert. I suppose everybody loves eating dessert, although my cousin Matthew doesn't. He never eats dessert. My Auntie Vera always said she didn't eat dessert, but we all just laughed at that because as soon as the dessert came out, she was first in line with a plate and a spoon. So maybe not everybody loves dessert but I think most people do. And yet it's not very good for us, so we all probably eat too much of it. I know that's my problem. I just love to have something sweet after a meal. And I keep on eating dessert, even though I know it's not good for me. But I eat it anyway. I wonder why.

Well, that certainly was free-writing. And while it certainly isn't any good, I think there might be something good in there. The part that seems most promising to me is the part about my aunt always saying she didn't eat dessert and then always eating it. Everyone in the family always had a good laugh over that. So it's possible that if I tell the story well, my readers might laugh, too. But on the whole, I'm not very excited by what I've done here.

ACTIVITY: PANNING FOR GOLD WITH TIMED FREE-WRITING

I've found that free writing works best when there's a little pressure on, especially the pressure of time. Set a timer for two minutes and just start writing. When the time is up, stop and read over what you've written. Now, read it over a second time and underline the best part. Next, take that one part, re-write it at the top of a new sheet of paper and free write on that for two minutes. Repeat this exercise a few times and you may accumulate enough "nuggets of gold" to get a good piece started.

ACTIVITY: BUILD YOUR FREE-WRITING MUSCLES

If you've ever lifted weights, run track, or done any other kind of strength- or endurance-building activities, you know that when you start out, you can't do very much, but that after a few weeks of practice, your capacity increases. It's the same with writing. Start with a one-minute free write. That's pretty easy. Then add a minute and write for two. Still not so hard. Then, try adding one minute a day to this endurance test and see how you do. If you get comfortable writing for ten to fifteen minutes at a shot, you will have developed some powerful writing muscles you can depend on when the going gets tough.

FREE-LISTING

Another way to do free-writing is to make lists. Some people find this even more freeing because they don't need to worry about writing in sentences. Free-listing usually doesn't work any better for me than free-writing, but we never know until we try these things, so I'm going to give it a try right now.

EXAMPLE:

Here's a list of things that popped into my mind about the topic "driving."

- Hate it
- Boring
- Dangerous
- Expensive
- Nothing to do
- Listen to the radio
- Getting lost
- My big car accident
- Getting car fixed
- Putting in gas
- Insurance
- Waste of time
- Never liked it even when I was a kid
- Hate taking the bus, too
- Maybe I just have a problem with transportation
- Honda Accord
- Would like to get a hybrid
- Gas is expensive
- Using maps
- Getting directions from the Internet

Once again, there's probably some good stuff in there somewhere. The trick is figuring out where it is. I found myself getting more interested when I got to the point where I wrote, "Hate taking the bus, too" and "Maybe I just have a problem with transportation." Maybe I could do something funny with this, but at the moment I'm not sure what.

Like the bit in the previous example about my aunt telling us she didn't eat dessert, I seem to have stumbled onto something that wasn't on my mind at all when I started but that might turn into something interesting. That's probably the value of most free-writing exercises: they help you stumble onto things you wouldn't have thought of under more structured circumstances.

TIP:

If you get into the habit of free-writing, you'll find yourself getting into the habit of throwing writing away. This is good, not bad. Most of us—me included—are simply too attached to what we write. When it comes time to revise or edit, we don't want to change a thing. But the most successful writers are usually those who throw out more words than they keep.

FREE ASSOCIATION

Almost every kid in America knows about this pre-writing technique, although most of you would know it by a different name. In school, you'd probably call this "webbing" or "mind mapping." Every teacher learns this activity when they get their training, so it's probably the most popular academic writing strategy ever.

Problem is, I've never in my life heard of a writer who has used it.

When I first started working in schools, I gave it a try. But after doing it a few times up at the chalkboard and seeing what the kids came up with at their desks, I couldn't figure out how we could turn what we had into good writing. So I stopped using it and have never gone back.

EXAMPLE:

Here I am free associating in the typical web or mind map style you know from school. The topic is "fixing my computer."

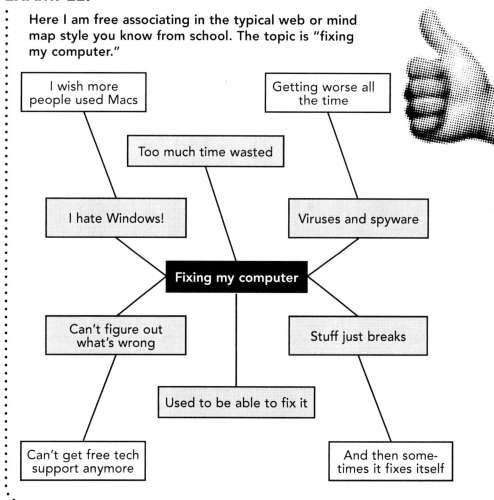

Now maybe if Spider-Man were your writing teacher, he'd be able to make this work. But for the life of me, I've never been able to help my students translate this into good writing. Maybe I just don't have the "spidey sense" for it. Or perhaps my problem is that I get caught in the web and end up putting more effort into making a fancy chart than I do into making good writing.

Then there's the time factor. It took me about ten minutes to do this. That's about eight minutes longer than it took me to do the other free-writing activities. And I don't have anything to show for all that extra time and effort. I also noticed that I didn't stumble onto anything surprising while I was doing it. I think the complexity of connecting things short circuits the freedom to put anything down.

I watch kids in school do these webs all the time. When they use big paper and different colors, they come up with some truly spectacular creations. But I don't see a lot of truly spectacular writing as a result. Plus, as I mentioned before, I don't know any truly spectacular writers who do this.

So, should you try it?

You're in charge of your own writing process. You pick the strategies and decide when and how to use them. The only thing that matters is that you pick things that work. How do you know if something works? That's easy. If a strategy helps you write better, faster, and more consistently than something else, it works.

FREEDOM ISN'T FREE

The problem I have found with these "free" approaches to pre-writing is that they tend to lull me into a false sense of security. I see a bunch of words down on the page and I feel like I've got a piece going. But usually, I don't. As the saying goes, "freedom isn't free." There's a price to pay for the ease of using these approaches and that price is something I call "structuring."

The beauty of these free-writing methods is that they are not highly structured. You can do just about anything you want and there aren't many rules. Actual writing, however, is the opposite: it's highly structured and has tons of rules. So even if I'm able to get a lot down on paper using these strategies, it's often hard for me to turn it into something I can actually use in a piece.

TIP:

A pre-writing strategy is only as good as the quality of the drafting it helps you produce. Trying different strategies is a way of getting to know yourself as a writer and developing your own way of writing. In school, we would call this your own writing process, but it doesn't really matter what we call it. What matters is that you figure it out for yourself. The best way to do that is to experiment and try different things. So read on, and we'll try a few more.

OUTLINING

When you get old like me, you realize the truth behind sayings such as, "Never say never." But just because something is true doesn't mean I can't take the risk of ignoring it once in a while, so here goes: I *never* use outlining.

Now, you might be thinking, if I never use it, why bother putting it in this chapter? Well, it's so much a part of our culture that I just didn't think I could write a book about writing without at least mentioning it. And in the spirit of knowing myself better as a writer, I'll even give it a try.

Here's an outline for a piece about how ridiculous it is that there are so many varieties of Coca-Cola in stores today:

1. Too many kinds of Coke
   a. Coke
   b. Diet Coke
   c. Caffeine Free Coke
   d. Caffeine Free Diet Coke
   e. Diet Coke with Lemon
   f. Diet Coke with Lime
   g. Vanilla Coke
   h. Coke Zero
   i. Coke C2
2. Why I don't like it
   a. I feel like I have to try each one
   b. It's too hard to just buy someone a Coke these days
   c. Stores can't stock every kind
3. What I think should be done
   a. Go back to Coke and Diet Coke
   b. Sell fancy flavors over the Internet only

In contrast to the free-writing strategies we tried in the previous section, outlining is highly structured. If I wrote a composition based on the above outline, I'd have a highly structured piece, but I don't think it would be a very good one. I also find the process of making an outline unsatisfying.

A SCHOOL TOOL

Outlining is something most of us encounter in school. When I was a kid, each of my teachers from about fourth grade on routinely requested outlines with any research paper we would write. My parents seem to have had the same experience, and I suppose their parents before them turned in outlines with papers, too.

But did anyone of ever really use outlining as a strategy to write more effectively? Perhaps a few did, but not very many.

When I was in school, the big joke about outlining was that most of us wrote the paper and then made the outline afterward just because we had to turn it in. Savvy teachers, of course, would request our outlines weeks in advance of the due date. But since most of us had just made them up arbitrarily without giving much thought as to what we would write, I think the task qualified more as busy work than as a helpful tool for improving one's prose.

To be certain, many people did make legitimate outlines in school and some of those may have even followed them when they started writing. I'm even willing to admit that some of these people found outlining useful and that it may have helped them improve their work. But in my experience, most people don't use outlining much, and even when they do, it doesn't make them better writers.

EXAMPLE: ·

Writers in the field of technical writing are inclined to use outlines because much of their work involves creating detailed inventories of information describing how things like computers work. Researchers publishing in academic disciplines, like math or science, are often required to use outlines. Many legal agreements require a numbered outline structure. And often, when submitting proposals or writing grants, the people who create these documents have to follow an outline created by the organization they are writing to.

One creative use of outlining in the world of fiction is this:
Some novelists, especially those writing in genres like mystery
or fantasy, which often have highly complex plots, will sometimes outline an entire novel after finishing a draft just to make
sure the structure works exactly the way they want it to. And
while film and TV script writers probably don't think in terms of
outlines, many use specialized script-writing software that has
outlining built right into it.

DO REAL WRITERS USE OUTLINING?

The answer is yes, but probably more as a project management tool
than as a creative tool.

Miss Margot says

I hate outlines. I hated them in school
and I hate them now. The good thing is,
nobody ever asks me to write them. The
closest thing to an outline that I do is
to make a list of the topics I'm covering
within a story. It's not a real outline, but I
still hate doing it.

INLINING

As a teacher of writing, outlining used to present a problem for me:
I could hardly visit a school without being asked to teach it; yet at
the same time, I knew it wasn't very useful to the kids I was working
with. I needed a solution that would address teachers' needs to help
kids structure their writing and satisfy my goal of presenting authentic
strategies real writers use.

After several years of telling teachers I didn't teach outlining (and
getting into a lot of trouble for it), I asked myself a simple question:
"When I have a piece to write, how do I figure out the structure?"

In the process, I discovered a solution: the antidote to outlining is *inlining*.

What I realized was this: I often plan pieces in sections, each one beginning with its own catchy heading. This "catchy heading" style is probably the most common way writing is organized in newspapers, newsletters, magazines, websites, and other short non-fiction vehicles today.

EXAPLE:

THE TROUBLE WITH COKE TODAY

Coke, Coke Everywhere But Not a Drop to Drink
I'd Like to Buy the World a Coke (But I Can't!)
Back in the Good Ol' Days
Ain't Nothin' Like the Real Thing

These are the "lines." Now all I have to do is write "inside" of them like this:

THE TROUBLE WITH COKE TODAY

Coke, Coke Everywhere But Not a Drop to Drink

I received quite a surprise the other day when I walked into my local ZippyMart to get a Coke. Surveying the cooler, I discovered no less than seven varieties of my favorite beverage—none of which was the simple bottle of Coke Classic I was looking for. How could this…

I'd Like to Buy the World a Coke (But I Can't!)

If I'm heading over to the store for a Coke during the day, I'm inclined to ask my wife if she wants one, too. This used to be a simple transaction: "Want a Coke?" I'd holler as I headed out the door. "Sure" or "No, thanks," would be the reply. And I'd trundle off knowing exactly what to do. Not any more. Now, getting out of the house to get a Coke could take days of interrogation by a trained professional. If…

Back in the Good Ol' Days

There once was a time when a fella didn't have to enter into deep philosophical exploration to decide on a simple afternoon beverage. When I was little, there was just Coke. We didn't even have diet. But now…

Ain't Nothin' Like the Real Thing

Call me a sucker for slick advertising but when I see a bottle of Coke on TV and the ad says, "It's the real thing," I'm inclined to believe it. The company tried changing the taste of Coke once, way back when, and people got so upset they had to change it right back. Now if that doesn't…

Inlining is simple and, at least for me, it combines the structure of outlining with the flexibility of free-writing. To begin inlining, I start thinking about my topic—too many kinds of Coke—then I quickly make a short list of sub-topics that go with it. Often I can even work a title in, too.

If I think up a new section, I just write down the one line I need for the heading and then I go back and fill in my copy. I can also rearrange sections simply by cutting and pasting in my word processor. If I'm writing on paper, I just put each heading at the top of its own blank sheet and write each section separately.

This inlining approach feels very natural to me. It seems to strike just the right balance between structured outlining and unstructured free-writing. It also helps me produce complete drafts very quickly, which is the whole reason why we bother to do pre-writing in the first place.

HOW COME I'VE NEVER HEARD OF THIS BEFORE?

To my knowledge, no one else has ever identified a technique called "inlining." So don't go looking for it in any fancy professional writing books. You should, however, look for it in the world of professional writing. That's what I did.

I asked my wife about inlining (she writes about 200 of these short non-fiction pieces a year) and she said this is similar to how she works, though she'd never thought of it as a technique or heard it named before. I think that's how most writers would look at it.

After talking to my wife, I polled a few other writers I know. I explained what I did and why I called it inlining. Some of them didn't like the name, but most agreed that it was similar to the way they worked.

Miss Margot says

Sometimes I have a lot of great information, but I can't figure out where it should all go in my story. That's when inlining comes in handy. I just write individual sections of the story and then use transitions to link them together, like a daisy chain. If I don't like the order, it's easy to move the chunks around—even if I'm using paper.

ACTIVITY: COMBINING FREE WRITING AND INLINING

Do you want to get a piece going quickly? Combine free-listing and free-writing with inlining. Pick a topic. Spend one minute coming up with a list of all the possible subtopics that could go with it. Pick the best three or four subtopics you come up with. Now, set the timer for two minutes. Pick one of the subtopics and free-write about it. Repeat the two-minute free-write for each subtopic. You'll have a piece going in about ten minutes.

BE A WRITER LIKE DAN WHITTLE

Dan Whittle is an attorney with Environmental Defense, a national nonprofit organization that links science, economics, and law to create innovative, equitable, and cost-effective solutions to society's most urgent environmental problems. Before joining Environmental Defense, he worked as a policy advisor to the Governor of North Carolina, as a lawyer and lobbyist for Indian tribes, and as a wilderness guide in Alaska.

Q WHAT KIND OF WRITER ARE YOU?

A I'm a lawyer and advocate; I write mostly to convince other people to think or to do something. Unlike a lot of lawyers, I don't spend much time in court before judges and juries. Instead I work to protect the environment by convincing Congressmen and state legislators to enact strong laws and policies. Often my goal is simply to make people aware of an environmental problem, like global warming or over-fishing. Sometimes I want to encourage them to get involved in solving those problems. This requires a lot of writing. Often I take complicated scientific concepts and data and try to translate them into plain English. I write reports, journal articles, testimonies, opinion pieces for newspapers, and draft legislation. I'm not a professional writer, but the nature of my job requires that I write professionally. In fact, writing is perhaps the most essential tool of my trade.

Q WHY DO YOU WRITE?

A First and foremost, I write to organize my thoughts. Writing helps me figure out what I want to say and how I want to say it. I'm most successful when my writing is persuasive. I write to motivate others to take some action, such as writing a letter to a Congressman, attending a rally, eating organic foods, or recycling at home.

Q

WHAT MADE YOU WANT TO BE A WRITER?

A I'm not sure I ever *wanted* to be a writer. As a kid, I liked to argue, but wasn't fast enough on my feet to win many debates with my older brothers. So I began to write down what I wanted to say and found out that my written arguments made a lot more sense. In high school, I was asked to be a cub reporter for the school newspaper, and that was really fun. That's when I really started to enjoy writing.

Q

WHAT ADVICE WOULD YOU GIVE TO A FELLOW WRITER WHO WAS JUST STARTING OUT?

A Just do it. Really. Don't get frustrated if what you write doesn't sound quite right. Don't worry if you have trouble finding your own voice. Keep at it. Make practicing fun. Write about your dreams when you wake up, make up a poem when you're eating breakfast. Take one of your favorite songs and write different words for it. Before you go to bed, write about your day, even if you don't think much happened that day. And read—newspapers, novels, comic books, poems, anything. The more I read, the better my writing is.

SPECIAL STRUCTURED PRE-WRITING STRATEGIES

By now you may have figured out that the kinds of pre-writing strategies I like best are ones that blend a small amount of structure with a healthy dose of freedom. So the rest of this chapter will concentrate on tools that I think strike a perfect balance between the two.

I would be thoroughly surprised if a professional writer anywhere had ever used any of the pre-writing strategies I'm about to show you. And yet, when I came up with these strategies, I worked very hard to make sure they were modeled after the work of professional writers.

Throughout this book, I focus on how professional writers write. The way I look at it, if you want to learn something, go to someone whose livelihood depends on doing it well. But the pros don't know everything. For example, some may not be able to remember how it feels to be a young writer just getting started. Also, most professional writers don't teach writing, so they may not have much experience helping others learn. In situations where I recommend things to you that professional writers don't do, I'll try to tell you why I think you may benefit from them anyway. This section on special structured pre-writing strategies is one of those situations.

SPECIFIC PRE-WRITING STRATEGIES FOR SPECIFIC KINDS OF WRITING

When I first started teaching kids in school, I immediately ran into a problem with regard to pre-writing: I knew only a few basic strategies, but the kids had many different kinds of writing to do. Even if one of the strategies I knew helped them with one kind of writing, it probably wouldn't help with another.

This got me thinking. What if there was a completely different approach to pre-writing than the way I had been taught? What if I could invent a whole bunch of strategies writers could use to make writing easier regardless of the writing they wanted to produce?

These are four of the best strategies I came up with:

- **Action-Feelings-Setting.** A simple strategy that works perfectly any time you have to write a single scene from a story, real or imagined.

- **Transition-Action-Details.** A more complicated, but still very manageable strategy you can use to block out a sequence of events in any kind of writing. It's great for telling stories, but it also works for writing directions, talking about historical events, summarizing, and many other sequential writing tasks.

- **What-Why-How.** So much of the writing we do requires that we make a statement and back it up. In school, we call this expository writing, critical thinking, or thesis and support. In the real world, it's just called making a statement and backing it up.

- **Content-Purpose-Audience.** You know all those superheroes and sci-fi characters that can change into any kind of object or animal they want? That's what this strategy can do. While its main job is helping writers organize informational writing, such as reports or magazine articles, it can morph itself into almost any other kind of piece.

ACTION-FEELINGS-SETTING: THE THREE BASIC INGREDIENTS

Every story is really just a collection of scenes that come one right after another. So writing a story, whether it's something from your imagination or something from your life, is really about writing scenes. As readers move from scene to scene, they rely on basic story elements to make sure they don't lose their way. A great way to capture those basic elements before you start writing is the Action-Feelings-Setting strategy.

In stories, readers always want to know what's going on; they want to be able to follow the action. They also want to have interesting feelings as they read; the rollercoaster ride of emotions is an attractive aspect of almost all fiction and narrative non-fiction. Finally, most readers seem to need at least some basic information about setting, including where and when things occur and what leads to what.

Action. Feelings. Setting. These are the three basic ingredients of a scene. So every time you begin writing a scene in a fiction or non-fiction story, make sure your readers get three types of information:

- **Action.** There's something important happening in this scene. If there weren't, you wouldn't be writing about it. Your readers are following the action closely. You need to describe it simply and completely, so people will know what's going on.

- **Feelings.** There are important characters in this scene who have feelings about what is happening. You want your readers to care about your story. The best way to make this happen is to show how the characters within it feel and why they feel the way they do.

- **Setting.** Readers sometimes get confused if they don't know where and when something is taking place. They also like to know about things that led up to what you're writing about.

 **EXAMPLE:**

I've got a story in mind and a scene from that story I want to write about. The story is about my wedding, and the scene is right at the end of the ceremony where my wife and I decided (seeing as we were getting married in a bowling alley) that we would end by bowling a frame together.

ACTION	FEELINGS	SETTING
My wife and I are moving toward the foul line, side-by-side in adjacent lanes, about to let our bowling balls fly toward the pins.	I'm happy that I just got married, but I'm also really nervous because there are dozens of people watching our wedding ceremony and I don't want to throw a gutter ball.	We're standing on lanes 12 and 13 of the Rock 'n' Bowl bowling alley in New Orleans, LA. There's a big brass band warming up onstage, and the place is packed with people partying the night away.

What I've always loved about this strategy is how quick and easy it is. Filling in the boxes was a snap; it only took a minute or so, and now I've got some great material to work with. But I have something else, too: in the process of recalling this scene, and having to come up with the three basic ingredients, a rush of other details came to me and I started to get a sense of how I want this story to be told.

EXAMPLE:

WHY YOU WANNA GET MARRIED IN A BOWLIN' ALLEY?

"Why you wanna get married in a bowlin' alley?" a friend of my wife's had asked us a few months earlier. At the time, I didn't have a good answer. But now, standing in lanes 12 and 13 at the famous Rock 'n' Bowl in New Orleans, I knew exactly why.

To seal our union, my wife and I agreed to bowl a frame together. Instead of asking for the rings, the preacher asked for bowling balls, and the best man and maid of honor handed them to us.

I looked at Margot and she looked back at me. We were both happy, of course, but also incredibly nervous. (Why *did* we want to get married in a bowling alley?) And then, as we'd agreed, we counted off and moved together toward the foul line: "One, two, three!"

And we let our balls go.

Mine shot out quickly heading straight for the right side of the lane. I prayed it would stay in play so I'd be spared the embarrassment of a gutter ball. Miraculously, it hung on, barely nicking one pin in the far right corner.

Margot's ball was headed straight down the center. I looked back over my shoulder. Dozens of people had crowded around to watch our ceremony. As her ball rolled slowly but surely toward the head pin, they began to cheer.

Crash!

Every pin fell. The crowd went wild. On a stage to our right, a brass band began to play. Our friends moved in to congratulate us. People we didn't know were giving Margot high fives for her bowling brilliance. Everything seemed as perfect as it could be. And I knew that this was why we wanted to get married in a bowling alley.

SHORT AND SWEET

Over the last couple of years, I've found myself attracted to a new form of writing that some people call "microprose." Microprose pieces are really, really, really short, some less than 100 words long. After reading them for a while, and beginning to write them myself, I've realized how much I love this form. So it's not surprising that Action-Feelings-Setting has become one of my favorite pre-writing strategies. It's the best strategy I know for capturing a moment in a small number of words.

ACTIVITY: AFS, ASF, SFA, SAF, FAS, FSA

Something that has always fascinated me about the Action-Feelings-Setting strategy is that I can present the action, feelings, and setting information in almost any order I want. Starting with the setting is probably the most normal thing to do, and starting with the action is good for getting off to a quick start. But my favorite is starting with feelings because of the way it pulls my readers in and makes them want to read more. Imagine a piece that started like this: "I don't think I've ever been as terrified in my life as I was on that cold December night." Doesn't that make you eager to find out what happened?

Give it a try with your own piece. Start by filling out the chart with the basic action, feelings, and setting information. Then, as you begin to draft, play around with it a bit. Start your piece two or three different ways, using a different part of the chart each time. For such a simple technique, you'll be surprised at how well it works.

TRANSITION-ACTION-DETAILS: A SEQUENCE OF EVENTS

You do this all the time. You recount something that happened to you. You tell a friend about a movie you just saw. Or maybe in school you have to retell part of a story you've read. Sometimes, you even have to write down the steps you used to solve a problem in math. All of these things are the same in one important way: they all involve describing a sequence of events.

When you describe something as a sequence of events, you can use the same basic structure every time. This structure has three parts.

- **Transitions.** These are short words or phrases, such as "Then," "After a while," or "All of a sudden." They help introduce each new action in the sequence. You don't have to have a transition for each action, but transitions can help your writing flow more smoothly from section to section.

- **Actions.** These are the actual events, or things that happened, listed in the order in which they occurred.

- **Details.** This is additional information about each action. For example, for each thing that happens in a story, your readers may have two or three important questions they'd like you to answer. These answers are your details.

Opportunities to describe a sequence of events will come up all the time in your writing life, both in and out of school. You can use the TAD structure in many different situations: when you make up stories or talk about events in your own life; when you give someone directions or describe how to do something; when you have to produce a summary; when you have to describe the steps for solving a problem; when you recount an historical event in social studies; when you document chemical processes in science. The list goes on and on.

TAD IN ACTION

If you're sitting down to write a story, there's no faster way to get started than to use the Transition-Action-Details strategy.

··· EXAMPLE: ·······

Here's a story about a kid and his dog. They're exploring while on a family vacation. Then something unexpected happens.

TRANSITION	ACTION	DETAILS
Last summer,	I went on vacation with my family to the ocean.	• We go almost every year. • It's fun because there's a lot to do. • I get to do a lot of exploring with my dog.
On the third day,	I was walking with my dog along a cliff overlooking the beach below.	• We were about 75 feet up from the beach. • We were on a path with trees and brush and big piles of rocks by the edge.
All of a sudden,	My dog ran after the animal and jumped over the rocks to try to get it.	• He likes to chase things. • I was amazed at how fast he ran. • He got close to the rocks, but didn't stop. He just went right over.
[No Transition]	I ran after him, looked over the edge of the cliff, and found him clinging to some brush by his paws.	• I was so scared. • I thought he'd gone over the cliff and had fallen all the way down. • He looked scared, too.

At first I didn't know what to do. Then,	I tried to reach over the rocks to pull him up.	• I grabbed a piece of the branch and pulled him up with it. • I just kept telling him to hold on and not move. • I could tell that he was just as scared as I was.

FAST AND EASY

Just by reading across the rows you can see that the story practically writes itself. To turn this into a more complete first draft, all the writer has to do is add a beginning and an ending. If he discovers that something is out of order, it's easy to move things around at this stage, too. It's also easy to add more detail. Perhaps the best part of all is that it only takes about 10–15 minutes to create a chart like this.

Miss Margot says

I love to use TAD to write instructions. When we travel, someone has to take care of our dog. I use the TAD to make sure I'm giving clear instructions to the dog sitter about what to do and how and when to do it.

ACTIVITY: SUMMARIZE A STORY FROM YOUR LIFE

Every story we tell about something that has happened to us is a summary. You can't possibly tell everything that happened, so you hit the highlights. The TAD strategy is the perfect tool for this. Draw a 3-column chart with six or seven rows on a piece of paper. Put the first thing that happened in the first "Action" box in the top row of the middle column. Put the last thing that happened in the last "Action" box in the bottom row. Now all you have to do is fill in the middle and a couple of important details. You may not need transitions at all; they have a way of taking care of themselves when you get everything else worked out first.

WHAT MAKES THIS WRITING GOOD?

Here is a story of an unusual day. Written by a natural-born storyteller, this piece does a good job of recounting an event with humor and a simple style.

Day of Destiny

It was a humid day in July, the sign at the bank said that it was eighty-five degrees outside. My mom drove me to The Smithfield Theater. I had an important job to do. The job was more of a personal goal. It was to make people laugh.

The catch was that if I could stand up in front of a theater of people and tell a couple of jokes then I would get to see the movie, *Mission Impossible* for free.

When I got to the theater, I was sweating like a pig. The librarian that signed me up was dressed in a clown suit. She said, "Are we ready to make people laugh?"

I feebly answered, "Yes."

➡

When I got inside the theater, a guy was already telling some lame jokes. Then, when everyone was seated, he called my name, "C'mon down Zachary Williams!"

As I reached the first step to the stage, I had about a hundred butterflies in my stomach. By the third step, they multiplied. But then, very abruptly, when I reached for the microphone, all of the butterflies disappeared.

When I was done telling the jokes, I didn't turn red or anything, I just smiled. I noticed the size of the crowd and, suddenly, I knew what I was going to be when I grew up: a comedian.

Stories about things that happen to us usually depend on two elements: the order in which we tell them and the details we offer along the way. I think this writer did a good job in both respects.

The story is easy to follow and I never get lost. Each part flows logically from the previous part, and simple transitional phrases help me see how it all links together.

I love the little details, like the part where he says he was "sweating like a pig" or when he has butterflies because he's nervous, and then they multiply, but as soon as he grabs the microphone, they go away. This is a good way to show us he's nervous without having to write the word "nervous." It also shows us that once he starts, he's not nervous at all. This helps support what happens at the end when he decides to be a comedian.

The only thing I think I'm missing here is the comedy routine itself. I would have enjoyed more details about the jokes he told, how the audience reacted, and how he felt while he was doing it.

WHAT-WHY-HOW: WHEN YOU HAVE TO PROVE IT

Isn't it frustrating when you're trying to explain something important to someone and they don't understand you? Or maybe you're trying to convince someone of something and they're just not buying your argument.

The same thing can happen when you write. But it's worse because you can't be there to clear up any of your reader's confusion. The only thing you can do is write as clearly as you can and make sure your most important statements are backed up with strong support.

When you've got an important opinion to express, and your readers demand that you prove your point, use the What-Why-How strategy. As its name implies, the strategy has three parts that work together to help you create well-crafted arguments:

- **The "What" (As in, "What do you think?").** This is your opinion. State it simply and clearly. Sometimes a single sentence will be all you need. You can also think of this as your main idea if you're writing an essay, or as your thesis if you're working on a research paper.

- **The "Why" (As in, "Why do you think it?").** Opinions don't just pop up out of nowhere for no reason at all. If you've got an opinion, you must have a reason for it, and often more than one. Can't think of a reason? Maybe your opinion isn't really what you think it is. (But then, that's just my opinion!)

- **The "How" (As in, "How do you know?").** As the saying goes: "Everyone's entitled to his or her opinion." But are you, really? Where's your proof? What examples or evidence can you come up with to prove your point? The "how" is the hardest part to figure out, but it's also probably the most important.

TIP:

The key to a successful argument is great support. You've got to be able to back up your opinions with good reasons and solid evidence. You can use the What-Why-How strategy to support almost any statement you make in almost any type of piece. It's also perfect for school when your teachers ask for expository or persuasive writing. It even works well when you have to answer essay questions on a test. (But let's hope you don't have to deal with too many of those!)

WWH IN ACTION

Below you'll find a young writer struggling with the age-old problem of allowance. You know the drill: some kids get it; others don't. Some get a little; others get a lot. Sometimes you have to do things for it; other times you get it for doing nothing. What's the best way to approach the subject of allowance?

EXAMPLE:

In this situation, the writer wants to pursue something more interesting and more thoughtful than the typical fifth grade angle of just arguing for more allowance. In fact, she thinks some parents give their kids too much. She's walking a fine line here as she creates an argument for what the best approach to allowance might be. She needs to be clear and precise to be successful, and that's just what the What-Why-How strategy is for.

➡

WHAT	WHY	HOW
Allowance works out better when parents think carefully about how much their kids should get, what they get it for, and what they can spend it on.	Some kids have so much money that it really isn't good for them.	A kid in my class gets $50 a week and he's always bragging about how much money he has.
	Some kids get money just for doing normal stuff or for not getting into trouble.	Our neighbors give their kids money just to stop being bad, but it doesn't make them any nicer.
	Sometimes parents take away their kid's allowance and the kid doesn't think it's fair.	My mom took away my allowance once because I didn't clean my room, but I just forgot to do it.
	Allowance is a good way for kids to learn about money.	I save some of my allowance every week so I can buy something really special.

ORGANIZED AND CLEAR

Though the author will need to add more to this piece during drafting, she can be confident that she's building on a strong foundation because her ideas are clear and her argument is well organized. The most challenging part about this type of writing is telling things in a logical way. Some of us just aren't logical by nature. Fortunately, the What-Why-How strategy is.

Miss Margot says

Just in case you think Mr. Peha is making this up, let me tell you something. We don't just teach WWH to kids. We also teach it to grown-ups. That's right. We teach business people to use WWH to write better documents for work. And it works for them, too!

ACTIVITY: ASK FOR WHAT YOU WANT

We all want things in life. And when we're kids, we generally have to ask our parents if they'll let us have them. This is a perfect time to use the What-Why-How strategy. Think of something you want—something you have a reasonable chance of getting—and ask yourself "What do I think? Why do I think it? How do I know?" Work out the answers in your head; then try it out on your mom or dad. You don't even have to write it down, as long as you can remember it.

CONTENT-PURPOSE-AUDIENCE: THE DEFINITION OF WRITING

Why didn't they just tell me in kindergarten? I went through a lot of school—about twenty years if you count college—and I never really knew what writing was. I knew it had to do with words and ideas, of course, but I never had a crystal clear understanding of it that would help me write more effectively.

Then I started teaching writing and I realized that the students I was working with didn't know what writing was either. But now it was *my* responsibility to figure it out and teach it to them. So I thought about it for a while, and this is what I came up with: Writing is the communication of *content* for a *purpose* to an *audience*.

Here's what I mean by that:

- **Content (Main Idea + Key Details).** The content of a piece is what the writer wants to say. There are two parts to the content: the main idea or, as I like to call it, the one most important thing the author wants you to know; and the key details, or additional information that supports and explains the main idea.

- **Purpose (Think + Do).** The purpose of a piece is why the writer wrote it. As we discussed in the previous chapter, writers want their readers to think something after they've finished reading, and sometimes they want their readers to do something, too.

- **Audience (People + Questions).** The audience for a piece is who the writer writes to. We always write to people. Sometimes it's a specific person; sometimes it's a group of people. And people always have questions they want you to answer. So, you can think of the audience as the people you are writing to and the questions they have about your topic.

The secret of this pre-writing strategy is that every piece of writing can be broken down according to its content, purpose, and audience. That means we can use it for any kind of writing we want. Even better, when we have a topic in mind but don't know the type of piece we're trying to create, we know this strategy will work because we know it works for all types of writing.

CPA IN ACTION

Here's a piece I've been struggling with. Truth be told, it isn't anywhere near finished (I'm not even sure I *can* finish it). In fact, I've hardly made any progress on it at all in the four years I've been thinking about it.

Sometimes we pick a piece that ends up being harder to write than we think it will be. We try and try, but it just doesn't come together. Yet we don't give up because we feel there's something important we need to put down on paper. That's how it is with this piece about me and my dad.

My dad taught me how to fish when I was little, and I absolutely loved it. And because I loved fishing so much, I loved my dad for teaching me how to do it. Fishing was very important to me from the time I was about six years old until maybe age eleven or so. These years were also the best years between my dad and me. We haven't gotten along very well for most of my life, but rather than being sad about that, I try to remember the times when we did. As a part of that remembrance, I want to write a piece about fishing with my dad.

EXAMPLE:

Now that my dad is nearing the end of his life, getting this story done has become even more important to me. Because I have no idea what kind of piece this will be, I'm using the Content-Purpose-Audience strategy to get it worked out. This is what I've come up with so far: ➡️

C	Main Idea	Key Details
O	My dad and I didn't always get along very well, but he used to take me fishing when I was little, and these were some of the best times of my entire life.	The time my dad talked me into going fishing when he knew they had just stocked the lake. But he didn't tell me, so it would be a surprise.
N		
T		The time he took me salmon fishing on a fancy charter boat and I caught the biggest fish of my life.
E		
N		On Sunday mornings we would go to Green Lake. He would bring hot chocolate and donuts and we would fish for hours. Mostly, we just talked.
T		
P	Think	Do
U	We might not always love our parents but we are always tied to them. Choosing to remember the good parts of our relationship, instead of the bad, helps us feel better about them and about ourselves.	Tell your parents what you love most about them and all the good things they have given you. This is really all they ever want.
R		
P		
O		
S		
E		
A	People	Questions
U	Kids who might not always get along well with their parents.	Why didn't you and your dad get along very well?
D		
I		What was it about fishing that helped you get along better?
E		
N		Why did you stop fishing when you got older?
C		
E		

A PLACE TO START

Writing about my relationship with my dad is hard. It seems so complicated and I never know where to start. That's why I'm starting with the Content-Purpose-Audience strategy. It's one of the best ways I know of clarifying what I want to say.

Miss Margot says

CPA is the strategy I use most as a professional writer. When I have a million stories to write, or even just 200, it's hard to keep them all straight. Using CPA helps me quickly figure out what I want to say in each one. It also helps my editors see what I'm going to do before I spend a ton of time doing it. That way, if I don't like where a piece is going—or if my editor doesn't—I haven't spent hours laboring over something, only to end up rewriting it.

ACTIVITY: USE A PART OF THE CHART

There's no doubt that CPA is the most complicated strategy we've looked at so far. But it breaks down easily into bite-sized chunks. For example, you can get a lot of work done just by thinking of the questions people will have for you and writing those down before you start. Or just think of a few key details and go with that. Even by filling in part of the CPA chart, you're a lot farther along than you would be with a blank piece of paper.

REAL-WORLD PRE-WRITING

Somewhere near the beginning of this chapter, I defined pre-writing as "anything you do before you start writing." I also showed you a variety of pre-writing strategies. And while I firmly believe that everything I have told you is helpful, I admit that I have not painted an entirely accurate picture of how professional writers deal with this stage of the writing process. So I want to take a minute or two, right here at the end of the chapter, to set the record straight.

To most professional writers, pre-writing looks like… well, it looks like living, I guess.

If you walked into a big city newsroom and saw a bunch of reporters talking on the phone, reading things, surfing the web, and meeting with their editors, you'd be seeing pre-writing. If you watched me reading over old pieces I've written trying to find something similar to the piece I'm writing now, you'd be seeing pre-writing. If you watched my wife looking over a spreadsheet full of statistics describing changes in the Los Angeles commercial real estate market, you'd be seeing pre-writing. Even if you watched her walk our dog around the block when she gets stuck on a story, you'd be seeing pre-writing, too.

For most professional writers, pre-writing looks less like a strategy and more like thinking, talking, reading, researching, interviewing, taking notes, or sometimes just walking around and trying to come up with a new idea. So if professional writers don't use What-Why-How or Content-Purpose-Audience, why should you?

Because these strategies work.

I've tested each one on real professional writing projects of my own. I've even had a few other writers use them. I also tested them with thousands of students in schools across the country. So while I know

I'll never walk into that big city newsroom and see a bunch of journalists running around with CPA charts, I know that if I did, the quality of writing in that day's paper wouldn't suffer for it.

I don't want you running around your writing life with a bunch of CPA charts either. What I want is for you to know what writing is and how it works. Strategies like CPA, TAD, WWH, and AFS will help you learn that. My goal in showing you these strategies is not to get you to use them every time you write. In fact, I hope that as you grow, you'll use them less and less, choosing to rely on yourself and your own writing instincts, rather than on strategies, to get the job done.

The reason I want to teach you these strategies is so you'll have good tools to help move your writing forward when you're feeling stuck. I also want you to learn them well enough that they become a part of you, the part that begins to think like a writer. Thinking like a writer is what professional writers do. It's what enables them to write every day on tight deadlines and still do good work, even on days when they don't want to write or don't think they have anything to write about. Using the strategies I've given you here is a great way to learn how writers think.

As I've said before, and will undoubtedly say over and over again, there are many ways to get your work done. The trick is picking the ways that work best for you. If you don't feel like using a particular pre-writing strategy, don't worry about it. But if you're working on something important, and you get worried like I did at the beginning of this chapter, think about trying one or more of the strategies I've described. If it doesn't solve your problem, you certainly won't be any worse off than if you hadn't tried it at all. The great thing about pre-writing is that you've got nothing to lose—except maybe the frustration of writer's block.

Miss Margot says

Except for one kind of writing I do (advice columns on dating, if you must know), I don't use any of the charts Mr. Peha is talking about on a regular basis. But that's not because they're not good charts. It's because after so many years of writing thousands of words every day (no kidding!), I have these charts in my head. My brain has been trained to think like that, so I don't need the paper. If you use these enough, you'll realize that your brain is doing all the same stuff you used to do with the charts. And then pre-writing becomes even faster. It's so fast sometimes you don't even know you're doing it.

Why do I do use CPA for my advice column but not the other types of writing? Because I want to make sure my readers get the answers they're looking for. It's really important that I'm clear, too, because I only have 800 words to answer the question, and some of the issues are complicated. Using the CPA chart helps me make sure I'm answering the question completely and not creating new questions along the way. It's awesome.

CHAPTER THREE
Be a Drafter

TEN THINGS YOU NEED TO KNOW
EVEN IF YOU DON'T READ THIS CHAPTER

1   The key to successful drafting is making sure you don't psych yourself out.

2   Don't let your self-consciousness keep you from writing.

3   Every writer has to deal with writer's block; it's a normal thing that happens to writers all the time.

4   Do whatever you can to maintain your momentum and not stay stuck for too long.

5   Re-reading your piece from the beginning is a great way to pick things up after you get stuck.

6   Working on different parts of a piece out of order will keep you going if one part gets tough.

7   It doesn't really matter how many drafts you do as long as the last one is good.

8   Sometimes when you're really stuck, the best thing to do is to take a break and come back a few minutes later.

9   Most writers benefit from having a particular time and place to write.

10   In writing, as in so many other things, success often has more to do with attitude and effort than with skill.

WRITERS, START YOUR ENGINES

When racecar drivers drive right up behind the cars in front of them, they do it to take advantage of the reduced air pressure that follows in the wake of the car ahead. This helps them go faster without pushing their engines quite as hard. It's almost as if the car in front is helping to pull them along. This is called drafting.

What's my point? The conventional meaning of the word "drafting" is something like "creating a preliminary version of a document." But all that tells you is that a draft is something that isn't finished. Big deal. You probably already knew that. What you may not have known is that drafting is all about being pulled into your topic and letting it take you somewhere you've never been before.

You've thought about it during pre-writing. You may have even written a few notes. Now go. Let yourself be drawn in by the power of your ideas. Get up close to them; put your fingers on the keyboard; open up the throttle of your imagination; and don't stop until you cross the finish line.

THE YELLOW FLAG

Sounds easy, doesn't it? Well, it's not. You see, a lot of us don't like to drive fast. We putter around the track at ten miles an hour and wonder why we never get anywhere. Then there are the folks who spend most of their lives with their feet on the brake pedals. That's self-consciousness, the feeling that what you're writing is bad, that it doesn't make any sense, or that it will somehow embarrass you.

Drafting isn't really about doing something; it's about not doing some-thing else. Specifically, it's about not psyching yourself out, not making yourself afraid, not worrying about spinning out in the third turn and losing the race. Because here's the deal: you can't lose. That's right. Drafting is like playing a racecar video game with an endless supply of quarters. If you end up in a ditch with nothing to write about, pop in another coin, power up your pencil, and start driving again on some other part of your topic.

If you feel your self-consciousness catching up with you, hit the gas pedal and outrun it. If you think you're running out of gas, come in for a pit stop: take a look at what you wrote during pre-writing; fuel up on some of the notes you made before the race began; then get back out on the track.

LISTEN TO YOUR CREW CHIEF

When it's not going well, try to remember this: it's a long, long race from beginning to end, and part of the trick to finishing in good form is keeping that in mind. Every idea is 500 miles long, and every writer has to drive around that oil-soaked oval again and again, one mile at a time. Sometimes you're inspired and the driving is a blast, but sometimes you're not, and the driving is no fun at all. Sometimes you're out there writing even when you don't want to be, even when it's hard, even when it looks like you're the last car on the track struggling to finish long after all the other drivers have taken the checkered flag and all the fans have gone home.

THE WAIT BETWEEN THE WORDS

I suppose it's nice that I can describe drafting as if it was auto racing; gives you another way of thinking about it. This is actually a writing technique called *metaphor*. In metaphor, we explain one thing as though it were another. We do this because the first thing is hard to explain all by itself, as it is with drafting.

Don't get me wrong; it's not hard to say what drafting is. We could just call it, "writing something for the first time, usually in complete sentences, without going back to fix it up too much." But that doesn't tell us how drafting works or what we can do to make it work better.

As much as I enjoy my little racecar metaphor, I think it might be useful to talk for a few minutes about what drafting feels like when we do it. This is the part that's not so easy to explain. Most of what goes on with writing happens in our heads, and most writers aren't too willing to crack theirs open and give you a look inside. But short of going in for surgery, I'll do the best I can.

WHAT DRAFTING FEELS LIKE TO ME

Most writers will tell you, I think, that drafting has a kind of rhythm to it, an on-again, off-again quality that is sometimes frustrating, sometimes pleasurable. To me it feels like "hurry up and wait."

I sit here with my hands on the keyboard looking at a blinking cursor, and I wait until a group of words forms in my mind. Then, the instant it does, I hurry up and type it in as quickly as I can. Then I wait for the next group of words. Sometimes I wait for quite a while. And this is the fundamental problem every writer faces during drafting: there's much more waiting than there is typing.

I'm not talking about writer's block here. That's different (and worse). I'm talking about the time that just elapsed between the first three sentences of this paragraph and the one I have to write next. For some reason, the first three sentences popped into my head relatively quickly. But then I had nothing. So I had to wait a bit until the fourth sentence materialized in my brain. Then I had to type it up quick before it got away.

At this point in my life, the typing part is pretty easy for me. I can probably do about eighty words a minute. But that doesn't mean that if I write for ten minutes I'll end up with 800 words. Not even close. The problem is all that waiting in between the words. The solution is making that waiting time shorter.

TIP:

WAIT LESS, WRITE MORE

Waiting for the words to come is such a common experience for writers that I would imagine just about everyone has a few thoughts on the matter. Here are some of mine:

- **Remember to breathe.** I know this sounds stupid but it's not. Our brains need a constant supply of oxygen to function properly, and our bodies need regular, slow breathing in order for us to remain calm and focused. But I'll be darned if I don't hold my breath during most of those "hurry up and type" moments while I'm trying to get a sentence down. Then, as soon as I finish, I relax and breathe again. Trouble is, if I've got a bunch of words in my brain, that breath-holding lasts quite a while. And that means I'm probably not breathing regularly. As a result, I need more time to get back to normal, and that makes the wait between the words longer. If I could just remember to breathe more consistently, I'd probably get more writing done.

- **Write and re-read.** I'm in the habit nowadays of immediately re-reading just about every few sentences I write. The way I get the next sentence is almost always related to my having retained the previous sentence in my short-term memory. If the wait between the words gets much longer than ten or fifteen seconds, I almost always have to go back and re-read the last little bit I wrote.

- **Read the last few sentences out loud.** Here's a fascinating thing: nobody, including me, does this, but it sure does work. I guess we don't do it because it's embarrassing, as though we're talking to ourselves, or something. But hearing your own voice out loud is a great way to get that softer voice inside your head to yield the next thought.

- **Use place-holders.** Here's something I started doing a few months ago. Often when I'm writing, I get an idea, start to type, then realize it's not all there. I used to stop, get upset with myself, lose the idea, and start all over. Now I just leave space and continue. For example, I might do something like this: "The house was _____ and _____, but I could tell that _____." How's that for a half-formed thought? But now I can take a second and fill it in: "The house was dark and drafty, but I could tell that the last person who lived there had left under suspicious circumstances."

- **Don't fuss over errors.** If you're writing by hand and you want to change something, don't take the time to erase it; just cross it out. If you're working on the computer, don't correct every misspelled word or missed comma. Get your ideas down first and then go back later. That way, you won't lose the rhythm of the writing.

- **Put down parts of sentences.** Often I will have part of a sentence in my head long before I figure out the rest. In cases like these, it's almost always better if I can get that part down first, even if it's just a single phrase. Words are easier to work with on the page than in your head.

MAINTAINING MOMENTUM

There will be times when the words flow so easily you won't even notice the wait between them. Writing will seem effortless and natural, like breathing. Sadly, at least in my experience, these times are few and far between. For me, the words come out two or three sentences at a time. And then they stop. So I think about how I can keep those little groups of sentences coming as regularly as possible during a writing session.

To me, successful drafting is all about momentum. It's about finding your way and then keeping yourself heading in that direction as long as you can. When I have momentum, I try to take advantage of it by writing longer and getting more done. When I feel like I've lost momentum, I'll do what I can to find it again. Sometimes all I need to do is take my hands off the keyboard and lean back in my chair. Other times, I'll just sit and look out a window for a few seconds.

I don't know if this is a good quality in a writer, but I tend to monitor myself a lot as I draft. I'm always asking, "How's it going today? Is this the right idea to be working on? Is there a different approach I could take? Would it be easier if…?" And so on.

The downside of monitoring myself is that it sometimes takes my attention away from what I'm writing. But the upside is that I learn a lot about my writing process and have become a pretty good judge of how and when my drafting works best. Since so much of the time we spend writing is devoted to drafting, it might not be a bad idea to reflect a bit on how it works for you.

Miss Margot says

It was fun reading what Mr. Peha just wrote because I almost never think about writing the way he does. Then I thought I'd watch myself a little closer to see how my process is different. I don't forget to breathe, but when I get jammed up I hunch my shoulders. I get tense. I don't write and re-read—that would slow me down and I like to keep my foot on the gas when I'm writing. So I use lots of place-holders, never worry about errors, and jot down lots of sentence fragments. See, we all have different ways of writing, but there's a lot of overlap.

ACTIVITY. HOW DO YOU DRAFT?

Take a few minutes to watch how you write. Start drafting and see if you can reserve some of your attention to follow what happens in your mind and body as you compose. This can be hard to do but very valuable. Try to figure out what you do when things are going well and when they aren't. Look for patterns that track your productivity. This will reveal a lot about your writing process.

HOW DO YOU KEEP THE MUSIC PLAYING?

Drafting has its highs and lows. When it's going great, there's no better feeling in the world than watching your fingers fly as the words stream out like a song on the radio. But when all you get is static, it's a different feeling entirely.

It happens to every writer sooner or later. You get started on a piece and things are going great, when all of a sudden you have absolutely no idea what to write next. And this feeling of being stuck doesn't go away in just a few seconds. In fact, it feels so permanent you couldn't write another sentence if someone paid you $100.

This is writer's block, and as far as I know, no one has ever paid a kid to beat it; you have to beat it on your own.

TIP:

Fortunately, there are several things you can do to get yourself out of this most uncomfortable situation:

- **Re-read your piece from the beginning.** Sometimes you just need a little kick-start to get going again. Scroll back to the top or gather up your pages and read your piece through all the way from the beginning. You may be surprised to find that when you make it back up to where you were stuck, you know exactly how to continue.

  Because I'm so afraid of being stuck at the beginning of a writing session, I begin by re-reading what I wrote the day before. In the case of this book, that means that each time I sit down to work, I go back to the beginning of whatever chapter I'm working on and read all the way up to the point where I need to add new material. This is time-consuming, but it really helps a lot.

- **Look over your pre-writing.** Get out the pre-writing you did for the piece you're working on and look it over again. Chances are you'll find something you haven't written about yet. And if you haven't done any pre-writing...

- **Do some pre-writing.** If you can't write, pre-write. With so many different strategies, you could probably pre-write for days. This may not be what you want to do, but a few minutes of pre-writing could help you get unstuck by helping you generate fresh ideas.

  The main pre-writing strategy I'm using for this book is inlining. When I get stuck, I look at the headings I've written and see if any of those inspire me. If they don't, I try to create new headings. From there, it's just a matter of filling them in.

- **Work on a different part of the piece.** One of my best writer's block strategies is to give up for a while at the point where I'm stuck and start in on a different part of the same piece. If you're stuck on the first sentence, this probably won't work for you, but assuming you've made it past the lead, it's a fine idea.

I think this is where my love of inlining comes from. Every subtopic I create is an independent section of my piece so can I work on them in any order. If one isn't going well, I just move to another.

- **Do some formatting, editing, or re-copying.** Another one of my tricks is to actually stop writing, but to keep working on the same piece in different ways. If I'm working on a computer, I'll take a few minutes and do some formatting. Even if I'm not on a computer, I can still do some light editing here and there, making small changes and cleaning up errors I ignored earlier. Sometimes, because my handwriting is pretty bad, I'll recopy some parts onto new pages so I can read them more easily.

- **Read your writing to someone else.** Almost no one ever does this, but it certainly can be very helpful. A great way to figure out what to do next is to have someone else figure it out for you. Share your writing with another person. Tell that person you're stuck and that you don't know what to write next. See what ideas he or she comes up with.

  This is one of the rare occasions when writing in school has its advantages. In class, you've got an instant audience. And if your teacher is running a Writer's Workshop where everyone knows how to share and respond, you'll probably end up with more ideas than you know what to do with. If your teacher isn't running a Writer's Workshop, and the kids in your class don't know how to share and respond, try to find an adult who knows you well and who knows at least a little about writing.

- **Work on another piece.** When all else fails, you can always put your current piece away and work on a different piece. Sometimes writers get so stuck or tired of a piece that they really do need to put it down for a while. Whether you start a new piece, or pick up an old one, it doesn't matter. Come back to your current piece when you figure out what you want to do with it.

Perhaps the best advice you could reflect on when writer's block strikes is simply not to worry about it too much. It really does happen all the time. Writing requires creative inspiration and sometimes you don't feel creative or inspired. In cases like this, most writers stop writing for a while. Sometimes it's just long enough to take a walk around the block or watch a television show. Other times, stopping for the rest of the day or even a few days might be required. The key to getting through these times is to remember you're a writer and to know you'll start writing again—just as soon as you're ready.

Miss Margot says

When I get writer's block and I don't feel like walking around the block or playing with our dog, I read. I pick up something by one of my favorite authors, including Mark Twain, Daniel Wallace, or Stanley Bing. Or I'll grab a magazine that's full of good writing, such as *Outside*, *The New Yorker*, or *The Oxford American*. Reading other good writers motivates me to go back to my piece, and the break in the writing action allows my thoughts to catch up with my keyboarding.

ACTIVITY: WHY DO I GET BLOCKED?

The next time you experience writer's block, think for a second about why you're stuck. Is it because you're out of ideas? Or is it because you're just tired? Maybe you don't like the piece you're working on. Maybe it's not a good time of day for you. No writer can completely avoid writer's block, but all writers can learn to avoid situations that make it more likely to occur.

BE A WRITER LIKE PHILIP DODD

Philip Dodd was a book publisher for fifteen years before becoming a writer and publishing consultant. His most recent book is The Book Of Cities, *which celebrates the culture and character of 250 of the world's most interesting cities. He has also worked with the Rolling Stones on their autobiography,* According To The Rolling Stones, *and with Nick Mason on his personal history of Pink Floyd,* Inside Out.

Q WHAT KIND OF WRITER ARE YOU?

A I'm a non-fiction book writer, so I'm usually writing about factual subjects after doing a load of research, trying to convey my personal take on what I've found out. I've written books on music—rock 'n' roll, mainly—and one about the great cities of the world. I also help other people write their own autobiographies or personal histories, which involves interviewing them and then turning their spoken words into text using their distinctive voice. I have also done some copywriting for design groups, supplying the words for brochures, ads, and slogans for their clients—anything from beer companies to restaurant chains.

Q WHY DO YOU WRITE?

A I've always loved words and playing with words—I still do, especially great puns (I just saw a delivery van for a Portuguese chicken restaurant which had "Poultry in motion" on the side). I enjoy the challenge of trying to communicate ideas, hoping that readers will come away with some fresh insight into whatever I have been writing about. These days I write because publishers commission me, but I never think of writing as a chore: every day I am learning new things.

Q

WHAT MADE YOU WANT TO BE A WRITER?

A

There must have been something planted in my brain early on. In my loft I've got a "book" I wrote when I was about seven. Winston Churchill, the great British Prime Minister of the Second World War, had just died, and I took it upon myself to write a biography of him, complete with introduction, chapters, and photo captions. As a teenager I created magazines based on my life—which was a pretty unremarkable one, believe me—and just carried on doing similar things. Now I'm lucky enough to make a living out of writing and editing.

Q

WHAT ADVICE WOULD YOU GIVE TO A FELLOW WRITER WHO WAS JUST STARTING OUT?

A

My advice is always "structure, structure, structure." By that, I mean try mapping out whatever you are going to write and plan roughly how many words you need for each section. When you've got all your thoughts and notes together, bash out a first draft, following the plan. If you can't think of what to write, simply put down the first thing that comes into your head, even if it's "blah, blah, blah", anything to fill the space—funnily enough, I sometimes find those are the best bits! The structure stops you worrying about the shape of what you're going to be doing—it gets rid of that "blank page" phobia some writers suffer from—and frees you up to get creative.

Also, read as much as you can—anything you like: trashy novels, great literature, erudite biographies, celebrity magazines, serious newspapers, etc. Keep pouring new thoughts, new words, new phrases into the reservoir of your brain to refresh it, and you'll find you're always full of fresh ideas and ways of writing what you really want to say.

WHEN IS MY FIRST DRAFT DONE?

I knew you were going to ask that. And I'm afraid I don't have an answer for you. Or, to be more accurate, I'm afraid I have several answers for you.

- **Your first draft is done the first time you get to the end of the piece.** In a perfect world, writers would pre-write and figure out a whole bunch of things they wanted to say about something. And then they would sit down and draft an entire piece from beginning to end and that would be a first draft. However, living as we do in a not-so-perfect world, this only happens when the piece is very short, or the writer is very lucky. Often, it can be hard to tell how far into a piece you are (don't even get me started on how hard it is to figure out when to stop). Also, you may not write it in order from beginning to end, preferring instead to hop around. That's how I do it.

- **Your first draft is done when the deadline arrives for your first draft to be done.** This is how it is on this book project. The whole thing runs off a schedule. I start a chapter on a certain date and I deliver a first draft of that chapter to my editor a few days later. She does her work and gets it back to me a few days after that and then I begin working on a second draft. My editor, who is also my wife, will tell you that if she didn't give me a deadline, I'd work on a first draft forever. I never think anything is good enough and I am forever wanting to make changes. I consider everything I write a partially completed first draft—even after it's published! But this doesn't go over very well in the world of professional writing, so I work on a schedule and turn things in, whether I think they're ready or not.

- **Your first draft is done whenever you say it is.** This is more my speed. As long as you can be honest with yourself, it works pretty well for anyone who doesn't have to deal with strict deadlines.

In this scenario, I feel like I've got a first draft done when I've produced the first complete version of the piece I set out to write. For example, I would consider that little piece I wrote in Chapter 2 about my wedding a first draft. It feels to me like a complete piece. And yet, I can already tell there are several things I want to change about it to make it better.

- **The question is meaningless.** I don't mean to say that the question is bad; it's not. But if you think about it, what difference does it make which draft you're on or whether you've completed a first one? If I stop writing right this minute and hand you this chapter, it's a draft. If I go back and re-write it up to this point seven more times, I suppose what I'd have is an 8th draft. And what if I never hand the piece in while it's still a work in progress? What if I never say, "Here's a draft of Chapter 3 of *Be a Writer*"? The point is, a draft is what a writer says it is. The only definition that means anything is yours—unless there's someone forcing you to write on a schedule like an editor or a teacher. Then the only definition that matters is theirs.

THE END OF A DRAFT IS THE START OF A BREAK

Here's something I do that helps me a lot: I stop working on a piece at certain times and let it sit for a while. For example, if I wasn't on a breakneck schedule to get this book to my publisher, I'd love to let this chapter sit for a few days, or maybe even a few weeks, before taking another crack at it.

In this sense, the end of a draft would be the start of a break I would take from working on this piece. I could stop writing at any point and then pick it up again later. How much later? Ideally I'd like to leave a piece long enough so that I could forget about it. When I pick it up again and begin a new draft, I'd like to feel as though I'm reading it for the first time, just like my readers.

One of the hardest things about writing is that writers read their words a million times but readers read them only once. After I've been working on a draft for a while, I know it so well I can't tell any more how it will sound to a person who is reading it for the first time. When I realize this has happened, I put the piece away and try not to come back to it until enough time has past that it feels new to me again.

Miss Margot says

Since I have to write on really tight dead-lines, I can't let my pieces sit very long. So I put them away for a few minutes, go back over them one time, and send them out. Even that short break gives me enough room to find problems I've missed, or improve things that weren't quite right.

KEEPING SCORE

This issue of what's a first draft, or how many drafts we're supposed to do, comes from school. Sometimes teachers will require a certain number of drafts, or ask us to turn in a first draft on a certain date. But when we're writing on our own, we don't have this artificial struc-ture, so we tend to invent new ones for ourselves. Thinking I'm on my third draft of something may help me feel like I'm making progress; nothing wrong with that. I just have to keep in mind that a higher number of drafts doesn't necessarily indicate a higher quality of writing. Sometimes the first draft is the best.

Then there's the tendency we all have to want to keep score. To most of us, being on our first draft is not as good as being on our third. Or maybe we're impressed when we hear a story of a writer who wrote ten drafts of a novel. But is that necessarily good? Does it speak to the writer's perseverance, or does it mean he just wasted a lot of time? Writing more drafts doesn't mean the end result will be better. It just means more drafts. That said, most of us really do benefit from cycling frequently between drafting and revision as a piece progresses. Ultimately, the number of drafts you do, if you feel like doing any at all, is a choice you make that defines your writing process. Figure out what works for you and stick with it until it stops working.

Miss Margot says

I said back in Chapter 2 that I liked to draft. But that's not really true—at least not in a traditional way. Just as I like to pre-write in my head, I like to draft in my head, too. I'll research a story for days or even weeks, so the ideas form in my head before I ever sit down to write the first word. But just so you know, I didn't start out doing it that way. Early in my career, I used to draft on paper (we didn't have computers then). That's the best way to train your brain to do it!

WHAT MAKES THIS WRITING GOOD?

Here's something I'll bet you didn't know: a lot of kids in school—both boys and girls—choose to write about Barbie dolls. And let me tell you, there are strong feelings on both sides. Few subjects inspire sharper opinions, as you'll see here.

Dolls of Doom

I hate Barbie dolls. The worst things are the commercials. They have annoying little songs that they run in the background while these girls are going, "Wow! Her braid changes color!" and giggling their heads off. I had the little jingle for that dumb "Pet Doctor Barbie" running in my head for two weeks straight. Why did the song stop then? They came out with a new one!

➡ My sister has this one where the legs change from that weird orangey-pink skin color to some sort of sparkly black when you put the doll in cold water. "When the water's cold, Barbie dives right in; her wetsuit magically appears on her skin!" Wetsuit, schmet suit. I tried spraying the legs of the doll with some cold water, and it looked like either a whole bunch of moles or some weird case of skin cancer.

More and more keep coming out, more "Dolls of Doom", as I call them. Sure, they're selling by the thousands. But they only keep them interested for a month, and then they ask for another, and the cycle goes on. Pretty soon, some little girl's room will be filled with Barbies. If that happens to my little sister, her room will cave in on mine, which is right under it, unfortunately.

When I'm old enough, I'll join the Army and get myself an M-1 tank or a fleet of Harriers or something, and raid Mattel. Or maybe I'll make them make a doll like "Militia Barbie" or "In the Navy Now Barbie." Pretty soon, all the little girls in America will be saying: "I wanna Barbie, not a GI Joe!" Down with the dolls! Nuke every Toys 'R' Us that carries them! Let the revolution for a Barbie-free America begin!

Right away you can tell this is going to be a fun piece. The title catches your attention, the lead is simple and strong, and the first paragraph takes you fully into the writer's frustration. How could you not want to read the rest?

And the writer is believable, too. He's got several good details that show us exactly why he's so frustrated. In a persuasive essay like this, that helps his readers trust his opinion; they know he's had real experience and that he's not just making something up.

Most effective of all, however, is the writer's voice. The writer's strong, honest feelings and consistent personality (outrage mixed with a sense of humor) let us know that this is a real kid with a real sister with real dolls that are really driving him crazy.

I think he gets a bit carried away in the last paragraph, but the ending is funny and I think anyone can appreciate the joke here of a kid who acts as though a doll is somehow making life for everyone on the planet absolutely unbearable.

TIMES, PLACES, HABITS, ATTITUDES

Writers tend to be creatures of habit. I know I am. While I carry my laptop with me all the time, and am ready to toss off a few hundred words at a moment's notice while waiting in an airport, the truth is that I'm very particular about how and when I like to write.

A TIME TO WRITE

I like to write at night after the workday is done. It's not that darkness inspires me, but that peace and quiet does. During the day, I may have to stop at any time if I get a phone call or an urgent e-mail from a client. The world is more active during the day: phones ring; people knock on the door; the dog barks. But at night, the pace of life slows down and that seems to be just what I need for my writing to heat up.

I also need large blocks of time, ideally three to four hours at a stretch. I think this is because I do so much re-reading. I'm a very slow reader (about 150 words per minute). I'm also a big re-reader when I write; I read every sentence over and over and over. So churning out a few thousand words a day, like I need to do on this book project, requires several hours of my time, preferably in a single, uninterrupted session.

Let me be clear: this is not the easiest way to do things. But it's how I do things; it's part of my writing process and, at this point in my life, I'm not sure I could change it even if I wanted to.

TIP:

You need to find the right time to write, too; every writer does. Start thinking about what that time is and how much of it you need to do your best work.

Miss Margot says

I write all day, but I like writing least between three and five in the afternoon. I think it's because I still think of that as after-school playtime. I would never start my homework until around five o'clock. So even now, years later, I like writing best during school hours. Sometimes I even write very, very late at night (like after midnight).

A PLACE TO WRITE

Writing is one of those things you can do just about anywhere. But there are always places where writers write best—and where they don't write well at all. For example, at this moment I'm writing in a hotel room in Phoenix, Arizona. It's a nice room and I have my laptop right here. But something just doesn't feel right. I've been here for about a week now, writing every day. But I can't say that I've had a single session that was as productive as I would have liked.

I like to write at home in my office. Maybe it's the big monitor I have. Maybe it's the comfy chair. Maybe it's the window I look out of. I don't know. Most likely, it's just the feeling of being at home with my family that makes me feel good.

How important is having a good place to write? Well, if my calculations are correct, I'm about twice as productive at home as I am on the road, even with the same amount of writing time each day. When I work in a hotel room or in someone else's house, I can't seem to get in the zone. It's not that my writing is bad, it's just that there's less of it.

Where do you write best? Oddly enough, many kids I work with write best at school. If their teacher is running a Writer's Workshop every day, they might find long stretches of time several days a week where they can be very productive. But mostly, I find that kids who like to write prefer writing at home just like I do.

TIP:

The next few times you're writing, take note of what's going on around you and pay attention to what environment makes you most comfortable and productive.

Miss Margot says

I'm the opposite of Mr. Peha. If it's too quiet, I can't write. I like there to be distractions and activity—music, other people, weird noises. When I have a lot of writing to do, I go to a coffee house where there's lots of stuff going on. In a weird way, it helps me focus better if somebody's sniffling at the other table and the guy across from me is fidgeting while the traffic whizzes by and the coffee machine makes that chhhhhhhhhh-hhhhhhhhhhherrrrr noise.

A HABIT OF WRITING

No matter where I am, or when I choose to work, writing goes better when I do it every day. This appears to be true for almost all writers. In fact, after "Write what you know", the most frequent advice given to writers is "Write every day." Daily writing sessions, even if they're short, seem to make a huge difference in the quality and quantity of work we can produce.

Given my belief in the discipline of daily writing, you might assume that I write every day. I don't. And if you asked me why I'm not more famous or more talented, I would probably admit that not writing every day is a big part of it.

When I was a kid studying piano, I didn't practice every day. And I didn't make much progress there either. Sometimes, when I'm sick and I have to take medicine every day, I don't do that so well either. I've simply never been a very consistent person.

So, when it comes to writing every day, I must beg your forgiveness as I commit the worst crime a teacher can commit and ask you to do as I say and not as I do. Even though I don't write every day, I sincerely hope that you will.

Miss Margot says

It's okay, Mr. Peha, I write every day. So kids, do what Mr. Peha says and Miss Margot does!

I guarantee that if you write every day, the quality of your work, and the ease with which you produce it, will improve quickly. And it won't take long—maybe as little as a week—before you notice a difference.

AN ATTITUDE ABOUT WRITING

Most people decide to start writing because they think it will be fun, and most stop because it isn't. So what about those who stick with it? What do they think?

There's an attitude most writers have that keeps us going. I'm not sure how this attitude develops or where it comes from, but I do think it's real. And I know it makes a difference.

I've been working on the first draft of this chapter all week. It hasn't been going well. I've found the subject of drafting to be tougher than I thought. I'm also traveling, so I haven't been able to write in my favorite place or at my favorite time.

All I know is that there's a feeling I have, a feeling that something needs to be written and that I'm the one who needs to write it. As near as I can tell, that's the writer's attitude.

Day after day, draft after draft, sentence after tortured sentence, even when we don't want to write, we do. Deep inside we know something needs to be written. And if we don't write it, nobody else will.

You have things to write, too, ideas no one else can put into words because they are unique to your experience. These things need to be written. But if you don't do it, they'll never find their way into the world. That would be a shame because the world needs people like you who are willing to share their ideas with the rest of us.

CHAPTER FOUR

Be a Reviser

TEN THINGS YOU NEED TO KNOW
EVEN IF YOU DON'T READ THIS CHAPTER

1 Every time we revise, we have to answer three key questions: What should I change? Why should I change it? How will I know if my piece is better as a result?

2 With any piece there are countless revisions we can make; often it's best to concentrate on just a few.

3 The five most important revisions to consider are main idea, beginnings, endings, details, and the title.

4 Revising your main idea is the most crucial revision you can make because it affects everything else in your piece.

5 One of the things that makes revision especially challenging is that changing one part of your piece often affects other parts.

6 Most of the enjoyment readers get from a piece of writing comes from the details.

7 Work hard to include descriptive detail in your writing; "showing" is almost always better than telling.

8 Try many different beginnings; the beginning is the most important part of your piece.

9 A good ending should never simply restate what you've already written; it should take your reader beyond what you've said to tell them why it matters.

10 Titles are much more important than most people think; choose them wisely.

TAKE ANOTHER LOOK

I've been dreading this chapter.

As a writer, I enjoy revising. But many professional writers I know, and virtually all of the student writers I work with, don't. Revision is difficult and complex. There are so many ways to improve a piece of writing; it's hard to know where to start and even harder to know when to stop.

Revision can also be demoralizing. Say you've finished a full draft, complete from beginning to end. It feels good to have finished something, and even though you know you'll do more work on it, you have a sense of closure and a feeling of accomplishment. A week later, you take it out again. This time, however, you look at it with a reviser's eye and it doesn't look so good anymore. You see things you want to change in almost every paragraph. It'll probably take you longer to revise than it did to write in the first place.

This is not an uncommon experience.

A woman once wrote to me asking for help revising two essays. The essays were extremely important to her because they were part of her admissions application to a prestigious university.

After reading her work, I struggled with what to tell her. It's not that her writing was bad. It's just that there were so many things I could have told her to revise and so many ways to go about revising them. I didn't want to give her fifty things to do and make her feel like she needed to start over. So I had to think carefully about the advice I wanted to offer.

And I need to think carefully here about the advice I want to offer you.

The word "revise" literally means, "to look again". And that's exactly what we do. We take out something that feels like a completed draft and we take another look at it. The hard part is answering these three questions:

1   What should I change?

2   How should I change it?

3   After I've made a change, how will I know my piece is better?

Sometimes it's impossible to answer these questions. This is when we put the piece away again, reconnect with our sense of accomplishment, and get a little distance from it. But when we take it out a week later, we're right back where we started: with an unfinished piece and those same three questions to answer.

This can go on forever if we let it.

And so could this chapter. I'll bet it could be 200 pages long. Maybe 300. That's probably what it would take to cover the subject completely. And even after all that I still wouldn't have told you everything there is to know about it. So rather than tell you a hundred things about revision, I think I'll focus on just a few.

I'll try to pick things that are important to me in my own writing and in the writing I read. I'll also include things my students seem to benefit from. I'll work hard to make good choices so you won't have to wade through what feels like a phone book just to get a few pieces of useful advice.

And then I'll probably go back and revise this whole chapter.

SO MANY REVISIONS, SO LITTLE TIME

Sometimes I wonder why I bother to revise at all. There are so many issues to confront; revision never seems to end. Perhaps most challenging is this: fixing one part of a piece often causes problems in other parts. If, at times, writing feels like a high-wire walk, revision is the ultimate balancing act.

But we can't let that stop us, so let's take a look at a draft of mine and explore the possibility of revising it. Remember this piece from Chapter 1? I really did draft it up while I was waiting for someone. And I haven't done anything to it since.

WAITING GAMES

Right now, I'm waiting. I have a meeting with someone and I showed up early. This happens all the time. But somehow I never get used to it. I'm not a good waiter; never have been.

I spend a fair amount of my time waiting. I think we all do. As a kid, I didn't realize this. Like many kids, I was impatient. I couldn't just sit and wait for things; I always had to be doing something. As an adult, however, I'm less inclined toward being active all the time. And I like to think that I can wait patiently the way other grown-ups do.

But I can't.

At times like these, I realize I'm just a little kid in a big body. I'm still just as fidgety, just as restless. I may not need to run around and yell and scream like I used to, but I do need to be engaged, mentally if nothing else.

So I make up games.

I solve math problems. I make lists. I think back through the book I'm reading (if I have the book with me, I read it). I think of songs I know. Or make up new ones. I try to remember things I was supposed to do but have surely by now forgotten, and I plan to do them after I'm done doing the thing I'm waiting to do. Sometimes I just watch myself breathe (it's harder than you think and an interesting skill to master).

I've often thought that since I spend so much time waiting I might use these many minutes to develop a useful skill or somehow become a better person; perhaps I could learn a language or memorize inspiring quotations by famous people.

But that would take too long. And I'm not a good waiter; never have been.

I look at revision as a kind of problem-solving activity. For example, I really like the title of the piece, "Waiting Games." But I noticed that I only talk about the games I make up in one paragraph. Most of the piece is really about how I don't like waiting, not what I do about it. My title creates an expectation for the reader that the body of the piece doesn't fulfill. The easy thing to do would be to change the title but I don't think that would make the piece better. Plus, the idea of making up games to make waiting more pleasurable is why I wrote the piece to begin with.

Another thing I like about the piece is how I repeat the phrase, "I'm not a good waiter; never have been." But I don't show you what that means. I think I need to do a better job describing what it's like for me to wait rather than just saying I don't like it. Often, it's details like these that make or break a piece of writing.

Thinking about that repeated phrase makes me think about the beginning and the ending. I like the way the piece ends but I'm not sure now that the beginning is as strong as it could be. I didn't think at all about the beginning when I wrote it, and now, as I review it with revision in mind, that lack of thinking is beginning to show. I wonder if I need the first paragraph at all; I could start with the second paragraph just as easily. But that paragraph isn't going to get anyone's attention either.

LET'S TAKE A BREAK IN THE ACTION TO BRING YOU A WORD FROM OUR SPONSOR

Did you see what just happened? I had a perfectly charming 300-word piece that probably took me fifteen minutes to write. Now I've got a piece of junk that will probably take an hour or two to revise. Perhaps that's overstating things, but I think you get the idea.

I believe the revisions I've identified would make the piece better, assuming I can make them without messing up something else. I know, too, that making these revisions would be a lot of work—more work than it was to write the piece in the first place. This is the challenge of revision. If writing is hard, re-writing is even harder.

So what can we learn from this? And how can we approach revision practically, so it doesn't overwhelm and intimidate us? One approach I take when I'm teaching is to limit writers to just a few really important revisions at first.

EXAMPLE:

Let's go back and look at the revisions I proposed for my piece about waiting. I only had to consider five things to figure out what I needed to do:

- **Main Idea.** I have to consider the piece as a whole. What's it about, really? What's my message? What's the one most important thing I want my readers to know? I did this when I thought about my title and how most of the piece didn't develop my main idea about the games I play while I'm waiting.

- **Details.** Of course, as soon as I evaluate my main idea, I have to think about the details I'm using to support it. In this particular situation, it was interesting for me to realize how little detail I had. I'm always telling the kids I work with in school about this. And sure enough, I have the same problem: not enough detail, in general, and a lack of descriptive detail, in particular.

- **Beginning.** In a short piece, the beginning can make or break you. If the only thing I did to this piece was come up with a great beginning, it would still be a significant improvement.

- **Ending.** Like the relationship between main idea and details, beginning and ending usually have to be considered in tandem, too. My challenge, since I like using the little repeated phrase for my ending, will be to make sure that I retain, or even enhance, this element as I make other changes.

- **Title.** The title in a short piece fulfills a similar function as the beginning and is almost as important. I decided early on to keep my title. Now I just need to make sure I don't change the piece so much that it no longer makes sense.

Looking at my revision plan this way makes it seem more manageable. Thinking about five things instead of 50 isn't so bad. And I seem to have gotten a couple of them right the first time anyway.

Miss Margot says

Often, I don't have time to revise. That's because most of the assignments I get are short-notice, so I don't have much time to do anything! And when time is short, revision is often where I cut corners. I'll read a piece once before I turn it in and figure out what improvements I can make that won't take long or require an entire re-write. This was really hard early in my career, but the more I wrote, the easier it was to figure out how to improve a piece quickly.

CAN I GET A HIGH FIVE FOR THIS?

To keep from driving ourselves crazy, let's focus on just five areas of revision:

1 Main idea

2 Details

3 Beginnings

4 Endings

5 Titles

This seems very reasonable to me. But it also seems helpful. In my experience as a writer, I've been able to get a lot out of concentrating on these five things. And the students I've worked with have made great progress, too.

The most interesting thing I've discovered about concentrating on these-five areas is that after a while, I don't have to revise them anymore. After years of checking my drafts to make sure these basic elements are in order, I began to do a better job of taking care of them earlier in the writing process. For example, I've gotten much better at knowing what my main idea is. At this point, it's rare that I even start a piece without knowing it. This keeps me focused as I draft, and staying focused keeps me from creating a bunch of other problems.

So I hope as we cover these five areas of revision that instead of just learning to improve a particular draft, you also learn to improve your drafting.

THE SINGLE BEST REVISION YOU CAN MAKE

I was presenting a workshop for teachers when one of the participants shot her hand into the air and demanded to know the single best lesson she could teach to help her students improve their writing. I had no idea how to answer her question. At that moment, I couldn't possibly imagine one lesson that could help any writer improve that much; writing is just too complex. But I could tell she really wanted to know, so I told her I'd think it over and see if I could come up with something after the next break.

For a few minutes, I thought about what I do when I'm working with a student and I only have time to work on one thing. And then it came to me. More often than not, I work on the main idea because the main idea is the most important part of a short piece of writing.

WHAT'S A MAIN IDEA?

You've probably heard the term "main idea" many times from school. But if you're like most of us, you probably don't understand it very well. I know I was confused when I was your age. At different times I thought it was any or all of the following: the title, the main thing that happened in the story, the main character, the topic, or something entirely mysterious that I would never ever understand no matter how hard I tried. So when I started teaching kids about writing, I knew I needed to clear this up for myself first.

TIP:

The difficulty I had understanding the concept of a main idea was not entirely my fault, nor was it entirely the fault of my teachers. It's a tricky thing and, in truth, there is no single, universal definition. So I just made up a definition I thought would help kids write more effectively. Here it is:

The main idea of a piece of writing is the one most important thing the writer wants the reader to know.

LET ME TELL YOU A STORY

Remember the one about the turtle and the rabbit? The rabbit, who is really fast, has a race with the turtle, who is really slow. The rabbit takes an early lead. He gets so far ahead he feels like he can take a break. The turtle just keeps plugging away, step by tedious step, and eventually catches up. Realizing he's lost his lead, the rabbit sprints ahead again, this time getting so far out in front he has time to catch the hot new movie at the multiplex. Meanwhile, the turtle, who prefers reading books to watching movies, keeps to his consistent, though glacial pace, lumbering along, putting one big turtle paw in front of the other. And so it goes.

The story ends, of course, when the rabbit, who shot out of the movie theater like a lightning bolt when he saw that the turtle had caught up once again, and quickly found himself miles ahead of his competitor, decided he was hungry and stopped in at Frank's Finish Line Diner for a huge plate of chicken fried steak with biscuits and gravy and a big slice of apple pie à la mode. Now, the rabbit and Frank have been buddies since high school and Frank knows that after a big meal like that his furry little friend likes to stretch out for a nap on the comfy couch in the back room. Well, you can imagine what happened: there's the rabbit, his big bunny belly full to bursting with Frank's savory vittles, sawing logs on the couch while that pokey old turtle ambles over the finish line and wins.

So what's the one most important thing the writer of this story wants you to know? Don't get in a race with a turtle? Don't see the hot new movie at the multiplex? Don't order the chicken friend steak and apple pie à la mode at Frank's diner? Most people say it's something like, "Slow and steady wins the race." In this case, the main idea isn't actually written in the story. But you can figure it out from the key details, the most significant things that *are* in the story that help you understand the writer's message or, as it is sometimes called, the lesson or moral. You don't have to hide your main idea so cleverly in your own pieces. If you want, you can just tell your readers what it is. But you have to have a main idea so your readers will know what your piece is about—or at least be able to figure it out without too much head scratching.

Miss Margot says

To make sure I have a main idea, I think about telling a reader about my story and him asking, "Why should I care about that?" If I can't answer that question in a compelling way, I probably don't have a strong main idea.

WORKING WITH YOUR MAIN IDEA

Because your main idea is what your piece is all about, working on it has a significant effect on your final outcome. This is why it's probably the single most important revision you can make.

When you focus on your main idea, the most common situations you're likely to encounter are:

- **You don't have a main idea.** In some pieces, it's very hard to determine what your main idea is. Often, this is because there isn't a single most important point you're trying to get across; there are several points, all of which seem equally important. Solving this problem is a matter of deciding which one of the many different parts of a piece is the one you'd like to focus on. Then, of course, you have to be willing to toss out the other parts, or at least not spend so much time on them.

- **You don't have enough detail to support your main idea.** This is very common. You write a piece where the message is relatively clear, but you spend a lot of time talking about things that are less important than your main idea. This is what happened to me, I think, in my piece about waiting. Fortunately, the solution in this case is fairly simple: just add more detail to the most important parts.

- **You have too much detail that doesn't support your main idea.** This is similar to the previous problem, but it's usually solved by removing details rather than adding them. I create this problem in my writing all the time because I get caught up in explaining something in great detail when what I'm explaining just isn't that important to my reader. To fix this, I'll either remove entire sections of unneeded detail or collapse a paragraph or two down to a single sentence.

- **You have the wrong main idea. I hate this one.** Sometimes I'll spend hours on a piece, writing in what I feel is a fairly clear and engaging way, only to discover upon re-reading that I've written the wrong piece entirely. When I consider the piece as a whole, and think about the one most important thing I'm putting across, I realize I want to say something different. Often this means deleting large parts of the piece or just starting over. I'm usually sad or frustrated when this happens. But admitting the problem, and getting on with my writing, is better than wallowing in my despair. Every writer runs into dead ends and blind alleys. We just have to live with that possibility and not get down when it happens.

ONE THING LEADS TO ANOTHER

Messing around with your main idea is risky business. Make one small change and it seems to ripple through your entire piece. Soon you might feel as though you have to change the whole thing. This can be discouraging, especially if you felt good about the piece before you started. But there's another way to think about it.

Any piece we write has the potential, with a few changes, to become a different piece entirely. Take my waiting piece, for example. If I take out the part about who I'm waiting for and put in more about the little games I play, it's less about the waiting and more about the games. If I downplay the games but talk more about how fidgety I get when I've got time on my hands and nothing to do, the piece takes off in a different direction.

Inside any single piece we write are many other possible pieces. Take this part out, put that one in, and voilà! You've got something new and exciting. Yes, you'll have a bit more work to do, but the reward will likely be something that is significantly better than what you were working on before. And as an added bonus for making the effort to revise, we often end up with several good pieces out of one.

IT'S ALL IN THE DETAILS

It was always the same thing. Every time I turned in a piece of writing to my teachers, they would give me the same comment: "Great ideas, but you need more support." After a while, I figured out that this meant I didn't have enough details in my writing. But I still didn't know what to do.

My problem was that I didn't know much about details. Specifically, there were three important pieces of information I never understood:

- **What's a detail?** A detail is the answer to a question a reader might have. Readers are very curious; they almost always have questions they want you to answer. While they may understand your ideas, they often want to know more about them. The more interesting your writing seems, the more they want to know.

- **Why do we need details?** If you don't give your readers the information they want, they tend to get frustrated. It's like being told the first part of a joke and not getting to hear the punch line. Or watching a movie and not getting to see the end. You want your readers to feel satisfied, not frustrated, so having the right details is crucial.

- **How do I put details in my writing?** There are many ways to add details to a piece, but all of them work on the same basic principle: take something that exists and add to it in a way that makes it more specific. To show you how to do that, I'm going to introduce you to two strategies: Idea-Details and Tell-Show.

THE IDEA-DETAILS STRATEGY

When I was a kid in school, I didn't really need my teachers to tell me my writing lacked detail; I knew I didn't put enough details in. Like most kids, I was writing just enough to get by—and often not even that much. I had a hard time writing anything when I was younger and I thought putting in lots of detail was difficult and time consuming. At one point in my illustrious school career (probably most of third and fourth grade) I remember actually being afraid of details. I prayed my teachers would only ask for one or two; sometimes I couldn't even come up with that many. If only I'd had a simple strategy for adding details, things might have been easier for me.

Years later, when I started teaching writing, I realized how easy it could be to add details to a piece. I didn't want the students I was working with to struggle with the problems I had, so I came up with a simple tool: the Idea-Details strategy.

EXAMPLE:

Here's a quick draft of a paragraph about our dog. It's not bad, but it's not very good either because it lacks detail.

> Our dog, Ursa, is a mixed-breed: half Black Lab, half Basset Hound. Because of this combination, there are some odd things about him. People are always a little surprised when they see him because something about him just doesn't seem normal. They sort of do a double-take and then they ask, "What kind of dog is that?"

The obvious problem here is that while I tell you "there are some odd things about him", I don't tell you what those odd things are. Let's fix that:

IDEA	DETAILS
there are some odd things about him.	• He looks just like a Lab on top, with the normal head and body. • But on the bottom he has those funny short Basset Hound legs that are less than a foot long, and those strange turned out front paws. • The lady who used to deliver our mail always called him "Short Legs." • When we go to the beach, he'll charge after a stick you throw out in the waves just like most Labs will, but right at the waterline he'll remember he's part Bassett and stop immediately because Bassets don't like to get wet.

All I do here is take the part I want more details about—"there are some odd things about him"—and put that on the left side of an Idea-Details T-chart. Then I make a list on the right side of all the things that go with that statement. Now, with so many details, I have several choices about how and where to work them into my piece.

A GAME OF SHOW AND TELL

You probably remember this from kindergarten. You brought in something from home, stood up in front of your class, showed everyone what you brought, and told a few things about it. That was "show and tell." But what if, on the day your turn came up, you forgot to bring something from home and you still had to get up and tell people about it? You'd have to "show" them what it was with your words by describing it in interesting ways.

In writing, we often say that "showing" is better than just "telling." Here's why:

- **Showing is more specific than telling.** You could tell a reader about the weather in a story by writing, "The weather was really bad." But it might be better if you "showed" readers what the weather was like instead: "A harsh wind whipped through the trees as dark clouds poured down buckets of rain that overran the gutters and sloshed up onto the sidewalks."

- **Showing helps readers make pictures in their minds.** As the writer, you know what you "see" in your mind as you write, but all your readers have is your words. If you don't "show" them what you're talking about, they won't get the same pictures in their minds that you have in yours.

- **Showing can be more interesting than telling.** You could write something like, "My dog is cool." Or you could describe all the things that make your dog that way and let your readers figure out how cool he is by themselves. This makes readers more interested in your writing because they want to work harder to figure things out.

TIP:

Showing is one of the most sophisticated techniques a writer can use. It makes your writing more complex and more descriptive. It also helps you discover new ways to say things. Showing is the key to rich and satisfying descriptive writing that sounds like the writing you read in the very best books.

Miss Margot says

Reading is a great way to learn about writing. As a young journalist, my editors always said, "Show, don't tell", but they never showed me how to show. So I started paying attention to how other journalists showed in their stories. I noticed that some used statistics, others used anecdotes, and still others used more colorful words. Whatever device they used, I saw that their writing was easier to understand because they provided descriptive details in different ways.

HOW TO SHOW

Let's go back to my little piece about waiting. I mentioned that one of the weaknesses I wanted to address in revision had to do with this part: "At times like these, I realize I'm just a little kid in a big body. I'm still just as fidgety, just as restless." So here I am telling you that I'm fidgety and restless when I could be showing you instead. To do that, I use the Tell-Show strategy.

EXAMPLE:

TELL	SHOW
At times like these, I realize I'm just a little kid in a big body. I'm still just as fidgety, just as restless.	• My foot starts to tap and my leg starts to shake. • Sometimes, if I have a lot of energy, I might even drum my hands on the table. • If I have a song in my head, I'll start to hum very softly, but often it's not soft enough and someone looks at me like I'm being weird. • If I'm sitting in a coffee shop or other public place, I'll start looking around for something to do. I might even get up and start pacing.

With all this description, you don't have to imagine what I do when I'm restless; you can see it. This is the advantage of showing: it puts the picture you have in your mind into the mind of your reader.

IT REALLY IS ALL IN THE DETAILS

Sometimes when I'm teaching writing in school, I'll come upon a class of kids who just won't write at all. Most of the time, I think this means they've had a hard time with writing and that it's not something they enjoy very much. I can certainly understand that; I've had a hard time with it, too. So I'll ask them if they can each write just one sentence for me on any topic they choose. Most will agree that they can.

While a single sentence doesn't do much by itself, a single sentence with a few details to go with it is the basis for a paragraph and maybe even the start of an entire piece. Once I explain to them what a detail is and show them the Idea-Details and Tell-Show strategies, they immediately discover that it's easy to add detail any time they want. And in the process of turning single sentences into multiple sentences, they discover that details make writing worth reading.

ACTIVITY: SHOW WHAT YOU KNOW

As hard as showing can be, most people are much better at it than they think. Try this, for example: Close your eyes and envision yourself riding on a rollercoaster. What's it like? People laughing and screaming. Your body being tossed left and right. Everyone putting their hands up in the air as they swoop down from the highest heights. That's showing. Instead of writing, "The rollercoaster was fun," you could write, "As we dropped like a rock from the top of the track, everyone put their hands in the air and started screaming like crazy." Try the same exercise with other "telling" sentences like "The party was fun," "The movie was exciting," or "The house looked scary."

When it comes to the quality of your writing and the enjoyment readers get from it, details are probably the most important thing. Without good details, most writing isn't worth reading because it's hard for readers to know what you're trying to say. Your head is full of things they can't possibly know about. The question, of course, is how to get those things out of your head into theirs. The answer is all in the details.

BE A WRITER LIKE BEN HIPPEN

Ben Hippen used to be very active in the arts, especially music and film-making. For a long time he wrote music, fiction, and articles about music and other performing arts. Then two years ago he set out in a new direction and enrolled in medical school. Now he spends most of his time studying and training to be a doctor, as well as working in a laboratory doing cell biology research—and it turns out that all of these activities involve a lot of writing.

Q WHAT KIND OF WRITER ARE YOU?

A I'm a medical and scientific writer. I didn't realize this when I started medical school, but language—in particular, writing—is a very important part of medicine and medical research. It has been said that the average student learns about 18,000 new words during four years of medical school, which means that learning to be a doctor involves, in a sense, learning a new language. And, like any other new language, you don't just need to learn to speak it; you also need to learn to read and write it.

Q WHY DO YOU WRITE?

A In medicine, we write to accurately record a patient's experience in a way that we can use to help the patient get better. Whether it's a single phrase describing a small cut or dozens of pages amounting to a detailed medical biography spanning decades, it's not very useful unless the important information is recorded on the page in a way that other people can understand easily.

The goal of writing in medical research is similar. Modern science involves investigators in laboratories all over the world performing experiments and sharing their findings in scientific journals. It's a very collaborative process, and a vital part of it is the ability of researchers to provide clear and complete descriptions of their experimental procedures and results that other researchers can use to expand the body of humanity's scientific knowledge.

WHAT MADE YOU WANT TO BE A WRITER?

When I decided to start training to be a doctor, my goal was to be able to provide the best possible care for my patients. During my training I've become more and more aware of how important writing and language skills are to becoming a skillful doctor. So, if I want to be a better doctor, I need to be a better writer.

WHAT ADVICE WOULD YOU GIVE TO A FELLOW WRITER WHO WAS JUST STARTING OUT?

The most important quality of writing for a doctor or researcher is precision. For example, it's not enough just to say that a patient is feeling pain. To treat it, the doctor needs to record a precise description of the pain: is it aching? burning? throbbing? stabbing? Is it "tummy pain," or is it "tenderness that starts in the lower right quadrant of the abdomen, radiates to the navel, and worsens when the patient inhales?"

Being able to write precisely is important not just for doctors, but for all writers. A well-written description pulls the reader in and makes the reader able to visualize what was in the writer's head, whether it's the correct location for a surgeon to make an incision or the beauty of a landscape that is home to a character in a novel. This doesn't mean that every sentence in a novel (or a clinical report) needs to be bursting with adjectives. But it does mean that, when you need to, you'll have the ability write a description that puts the reader in the scene.

FIRST IMPRESSIONS

Has this ever happened to you? You pick up something to read, scan a paragraph or two, and then decide to put it down because it doesn't seem like something you want to spend your time on. Of course it has! We've all had that experience.

Readers don't want to waste their time reading something that doesn't interest them. One way readers determine their level of interest is by reading the beginning and seeing if they like it.

When you think about creating a good beginning for a piece, there are three important criteria you want to meet:

- **Catch the reader's attention.** Somewhere in your first paragraph, maybe even in the first sentence, you've got to come up with something that hooks your reader, something that says, "Hey, this is a good piece you're really going to enjoy!"

- **Make the reader want to read more.** It's not enough just to hook your reader, you've got to reel him in and get him to read the rest of your piece. Your beginning has to have something in it that makes your reader curious about what's coming up next.

- **Write appropriately for your purpose and audience.** Readers want to feel like the beginning of your piece is an invitation to an interesting and enjoyable experience. You don't want to start your piece in a way that makes people feel disrespected. You also don't want them to feel that you're just wasting their time or being silly.

The beginning is the most important part of a piece of writing. Why? Because if the beginning isn't good, many readers might not stick around for the middle or the end. Readers can be extremely judgmental. They are quick to evaluate a piece as being good, bad, or in between. And they often make that evaluation after reading just a few sentences.

Don't let them get away. Give them a beginning that keeps them glued to your every word. Give them a beginning that reaches out, grabs them by the collar, gives them a good strong shake, and says, "Hey you, reader! You need to read this!"

Miss Margot says

In journalism, we call beginnings ledes. I know; it's spelled funny. (Some people, like Mr. Peha, write it as "lead", like leader.) The lede is your beginning: the first sentence or paragraph that gets the reader engaged. In journalism, we don't have as long as a book writer might, so we have to get you interested in a very short amount of time with something that really grabs you.

ACTIVITY: HOW LONG IS A LEAD?

Take a look at a newspaper or magazine article. Read the beginning and ask yourself how long it takes the writer to really get into the story. People often ask me, "How long is a lead?" and the answer is, "as short as possible and as long as it needs to be." As a writer, I try to keep it to a minimum but from the reader's perspective, the lead won't feel finished until the story has begun.

BUT HOW DO I COME UP WITH A GOOD BEGINNING?

Since I've just made the case for how important beginnings are, it's fair to ask how you might come up with one or two yourself. Instead, I'm going to teach you how to come up with hundreds.

Here's the secret: steal them from other writers.

Take the beginning of this book, for example: "I hate writing. But I love having written." In my writer's imagination, of course, I have this image of someone taking my book down from a bookstore shelf, opening to the first page, reading those two lines, and having their wallet jump out of their back pocket and lead them to the sales counter. This will never happen, of course, but I chose those opening lines with the hope that they would at least communicate to potential readers that this was no ordinary book about writing and that I was going to try to get to the heart of what it means to be a writer, even when complexity and contradiction are involved.

Why couldn't you use this same opening strategy for a piece of yours? Just find the pattern ("I hate _____. But I love _____.") and replace it with content that goes with a piece of your own. For example, let's say you're writing a piece about your contradictory attitudes toward cooking and eating. You might come up with something like this: "I hate cooking. But I love eating a good meal." Or perhaps you're writing a piece about how you spend your weekends. You could start out like this: "I love sleeping in late on the weekend. But I hate how it messes up my schedule for the rest of the week." Here we turned the pattern around, but it still worked.

Miss Margot says

All good writers steal devices from other writers. A device is what Mr. Peha just showed you: "I hate ____. But I love ____." That's a good technique. But you don't want to steal too much from other writers. That's a bad technique with a very fancy name: plagiarism. It's even kind of hard to say, which should tell you how bad it is. You don't ever want to use whole sentences (or more) from other writers because then you're not actually writing; you're stealing.

GOOD BEGINNINGS ARE EVERYWHERE

There's a good beginning at the beginning of just about every book you read. Chapter books usually have a good beginning for every chapter. Every newspaper and magazine article has to have a good beginning to keep readers from moving to a different piece in the same publication. Even this book has good beginnings all over the place—or at least I hope it does.

In creating *Be a Writer,* I've chosen to organize my ideas into about 100 short sections. For each one, I've tried to come up with a beginning that I think will get your attention and make you want to read more.

EXAMPLE:

Let's look at the beginnings I've used so far in this chapter and analyze what I've been up to:

- *I've been dreading this chapter.*

  I call this a "strong feelings" beginning. For me, this is one of the easiest and most effective beginnings I can use. It usually startles readers to some degree because they're not normally accustomed to being hit with direct emotion at the top of a piece. It tends to make readers want to read more because once they understand how you're feeling, they can't help but want to find out why you feel the way you do.

- *Sometimes I wonder why I bother to revise at all.*

  I call this a "startling statement" beginning. You're reading a chapter about revising in a book devoted to making writing more successful and more satisfying. You don't expect to see such a discouraging statement right off the bat. After all, I'm supposed to be telling you why revision is important and how you can get better at it. Hopefully, you'll be surprised enough to read more.

- *I was presenting a workshop for teachers when one of the participants shot her hand into the air and demanded to know the single best lesson she could teach to help her students improve their writing.*

I call this an "action" beginning. Before you know it, you're thrust right into the action of a scene. In this case, I hope you can tell, by my choice of the verbs "shot" and "demanded", what an unusual occurrence this was for me and how surprised and even intimidated I was to get this question. When you're telling a story, you can't go wrong by starting right in with the action.

- *It was always the same thing. Every time I turned in a piece of writing to my teachers, they would give me the same comment: "Great ideas, but you need more support."*

I call this a "that's just like me" beginning. What I'm hoping here is that you'll read about my experience as a writer in school and immediately think, "Wow, that's just like me!" If you do, I've got you hooked. But even if you don't, I'm hoping you can at least connect with how it felt for me to be an unsuccessful writer when I was in school.

- *Has this ever happened to you? You pick up something to read, scan a paragraph or two, and then decide to put it down.*

The "question" beginning is one of the simplest of all. It's so easy you could do one for almost every piece. But please don't. It gets old fast. It does, however, work well and sometimes it's the perfect way to get something going.

The easiest way to get started writing your own good beginnings is to use models you already have in front of you. It isn't considered cheating to model your words after those of another writer, so don't worry about that. Just don't copy too many words exactly. Find the pattern you want to use in someone else's model and substitute new words into that pattern that match your ideas and make the writing your own.

Models are a great resource for you. They'll always give you something to think about when you're stuck. And, as you become more familiar with them, they'll become easier to use.

You'll probably find that you end up being better at some kinds of beginnings than you are at others. That's normal. You may also find that you like to change your beginnings in certain ways that are different from the models. That's cool, too. The models are just a starting point. Where you end up is up to you.

TIPS FOR GOOD BEGINNINGS

In my opinion, you can never get enough advice about good beginnings, so here's a little more:

- **Try several beginnings for each piece.** I almost always advise writers to try several different beginnings for each piece they write. If this seems to you like extra work, that's because it is. But it's really worth it. As I've said before, the beginning is the most important part of your piece, and you may not necessarily be in the best position to know which beginning is most effective. So what I usually suggest is this: try at least three different beginnings. Read them to other people and let your audience tell you which is most effective. Even if you already have a favorite, get this feedback from your audience. You don't have to do what they want. But it's always good to take others' opinions into consideration.

- **Reread, rethink, revise.** Once you have a beginning you like, look it over closely. Read it to yourself many times. Look for small ways to make it better. Change a word here or there. Improve the punctuation. Give the beginning of your piece extra care and attention, so it comes out just right. And don't forget to share it with others to get their opinions, too.

- **Variety is the spice of life.** After a while, you will find that some beginnings come quite easily to you — so easily you may want to use them over and over on every piece you write. Resist this temptation. In the first place, your readers will really appreciate it if you use many different kinds of beginnings. In the second, each kind of beginning you master makes you a better writer.

- **Start your own collection.** Ultimately, you'll want to move away from using the models I've presented here and start thinking about your own models. What kinds of beginnings do you like? Why do you like them? Which ones do your readers respond to most favorably? When you read a beginning you like, copy it down. For each beginning you collect, give it a name that describes how it works. Then write a few words about why you think it's good. One of the best ways to learn to write is to model your writing after the work of other writers you enjoy.

Miss Margot says

Every time I find a good example of writing I like, I make a copy of it. It might be a lede, a sentence, a way of adding detail, or just a pattern I enjoy. I make a note about what made me pull this example, and then I put it in a file folder I call my "Swipe File." I've been doing this for years and have quite a few folders! Whenever I'm feeling stuck, I flip through these folders and always find something that gets me unstuck, something that helps me not only finish my piece, but become a better writer in the process.

BEGINNINGS THAT SHOULD PROBABLY NEVER BE USED

Without disparaging in any way, shape, or form the creative genius of any writer living, dead, or hereafter to be born, I respectfully request that certain beginnings no longer be used.

- **The "telephone call" beginning.** "Hi! My name is Steve. Blah, blah, blah..."

  Unless I'm calling people on the phone to get them to buy something from me, or writing a piece about telemarketing, there is no reason why this beginning should ever be used. Most readers don't need to know the writer's name in order to understand the piece. And if they do, it belongs in the byline, not in the lead.

- **The completely unnecessary beginning.** "In this paper, I will be telling you about blah, blah, blah..."

  I should always trust that my readers are smart enough to figure out on their own what my piece is about. Telling them ahead of time doesn't win me any points. And, if my piece turns out to be about something different, then I've really gotten myself into a pickle, haven't I?

- **The "non-beginning" beginning.** "One day, blah, blah, blah..."

  While this may be the well-intentioned opening of many an earnest yarn, it is not a proper beginning. It doesn't do anything; it just sits there on the page, staring at us, thinking, "Couldn't come up with a real beginning, could you?" We could all spare ourselves this indignity by simply trying any other beginning at all. Similarly weak variations on the "non-beginning" beginning include "Once..." and "One time..." Not quite as bad, but still unexciting, the following beginnings may be used on an extremely limited basis and only in desperate situations: "Last year...", "Last week...", "A year ago...", "Last month...", "A month ago...", "A week ago...", "A day ago...", "A few days ago...", "A couple of days ago...", and so on.

YOU KNOW WHAT THEY SAY

There's an old saying that goes something like this: "You never get a second chance to make a first impression." Readers are only human, after all, and as such they're very impressionable. Get their attention with your first few words, and you're likely to hold it for another few hundred; hook 'em with a great first chapter, and they'll probably stick around to read the rest of your book. But the reverse is also true. If your beginning doesn't get their attention and make them want to read more, they may not get past the first paragraph.

Miss Margot says

I start every story the same way. Now, wait a minute! Didn't Mr. Peha just say not to do that? Yes, he did. But here's what I mean. Whenever I'm writing a story, I start by asking myself the same three questions: What's the news here? What's the story behind it? Why should I care? See, the questions are always the same, but the answers are always different. Asking these questions ensures I'm getting to the point quickly and giving my readers a reason to read the piece before they feel like not reading it.

LASTING MEMORIES

I'll tell you something right up front: endings are hard. Everybody struggles with them. Some writers rewrite their endings twenty times; others struggle with endings so much they don't even get a piece finished. That's just the way it is. Of course, there are things we can do to make it easier. That's what we're going to talk about here. But make no mistake; for most of us, endings are the hardest part of writing.

When you're trying to come up with a good ending for a piece, there are three things you need to think about. A good ending should:

- **Feel finished.** A good ending has a certain feeling to it, and that feeling is one of completeness. Complete means there's nothing else the writer needs to say; the piece has been wrapped up, summed up, and tied up so thoroughly that the reader feels completely satisfied.

- **Give the reader something to think about or do.** Readers like to ponder a bit at the end of a piece. In particular, they like to have something significant to consider, to reflect on, to carry into the future. Ideally, the writer's final thoughts become the reader's final thoughts and linger in the mind long after the last sentence has been read. That's the test of truly effective writing.

- **Meet your reader's expectations.** With the beginning and middle of your piece, you've set up certain expectations in the minds of your readers. Your ending has to live up to those expectations; it has to fulfill the promise of what has come before.

Too often, readers feel let down by the ending and that can ruin their entire experience. It's not that readers are mean people with impossibly high standards. In fact, it's quite the opposite. Your readers want you to have a great ending so badly they often can't help but disappoint themselves. This is just another reason why endings are so important and why good endings are so hard to write.

Miss Margot says

I rock at beginnings, but I'm terrible at endings. For me, endings are the hardest part of the story to write. I don't know why. Maybe it's because I'm tired at the end of a piece. Whatever the reason, I really struggle with endings. So don't feel bad if you do, too.

WHY ENDINGS ARE HARDER THAN BEGINNINGS

We can learn about endings the same way we learn about beginnings: by studying how they are used in the texts we read. But somehow it isn't as easy. For one thing, beginnings come at the beginning, so there's nothing else about the piece we have to think about. This means we can consider the beginning out of context; that is, we don't have to understand how it works with the rest of the writing. Endings, however, are written to work specifically with everything that has already been written. This means that an ending we like in a piece of someone else's can't easily be appropriated for a piece of our own.

There's another reason why endings are so much harder than beginnings. At the beginning of a piece, writers can do just about anything they want because readers have no expectations about what should or shouldn't be said. By the time the end rolls around, however, a writer's choices are constrained by everything that has been written up to that point. While almost any kind of beginning can work for almost any kind of piece, endings are specific to the pieces they are written for.

THINK, DO, FEEL, FUTURE

What's a struggling writer to do when it comes to endings? As I've thought about this over the years, and struggled myself as both a writer and a teacher of writing, one of the best ideas I've had is to think about endings as fitting into four broad categories:

- **"Think" endings.** In many cases, writers end their pieces with a specific bit of information they want you to go away thinking about. For example, at the end of the previous section on good beginnings, I ended with this: "If your beginning doesn't get their attention and make them want to read more, it's unlikely they'll get past the first paragraph." After all the information I gave you about beginnings, that's the little tidbit of wisdom I want you to come away with and think about at the end.

- **"Do" endings.** A common type of ending is the "Call to Action." In this approach, the writer uses the last sentence or two to ask the reader to do something. The ending of "Dolls of Doom" in Chapter 3 is a kind of "do" ending: "Down with the dolls! Nuke every Toys 'R' Us that carries them! Let the revolution for a Barbie-free America begin!" This kind of ending is used a lot in what your teachers call persuasive writing.

- **"Feel" endings.** I don't know why this kind of ending works; I just know that it does. Ending a piece with a statement about how you or someone else feels can be very effective. There's something about a profound feeling at the end of a piece that seems to wrap everything up. For example, in the piece, "Chores" from Chapter 1, the writer ends by telling us her overall feeling about doing chores: "Chores aren't the worst but they're definitely not the best."

- **"Future" endings.** As we read a piece, our natural inclination is to wonder what's coming up next. Of course, when we get to the end there is no next. But that doesn't stop us from wondering. It's natural, then, to write an ending that hints at the future. This allows the writer to end the piece while at the same time giving the reader a satisfying sense of things to come. The piece, "Day of Destiny" from Chapter 2 has a "future" ending: "When I was done telling the jokes I didn't turn red or anything, I just smiled. I noticed the size of the crowd and unexpectedly, I knew what I was going to be when I grew up: a comedian."

TIP:

There are many different kinds of endings and what you decide to call them doesn't matter as long as you can remember what they are. The important thing is to find ones that interest you and analyze them a bit. Why do you like some better than others? How and why do they work? Are they specific to one particular piece? Or could they be used as patterns for many different pieces? Do certain kinds of readers like certain kinds of endings? And so on.

Miss Margot says

Whenever I'm about to give up on an ending, I fall back on the "Think" strategy. It's the easiest one for me to write. The "Do" isn't a bad one either. But I'm going to experiment with the other ones Mr. Peha suggests the next time I can't figure out how to end a story.

THE "SO WHAT?"

Dr. Tony Canedo, former chairman of the English Department at Central Washington University, and one of my favorite teachers of all time, was the first person to ever teach me anything useful about writing. And what he taught me about writing endings has stayed with me for over twenty years now.

As sheepish undergraduates, my classmates and I would wait nervously to get our papers back from Dr. Canedo, and often our nervousness was justified. Dr. Canedo had very high standards; he not only wanted us to think clearly and to write well, he also wanted us to say something important. It wasn't enough in his class simply to describe some clever idea you'd come up with. You had to go a little farther, and come up with the "So what?"

At the end of our papers, most of us were making the basic grade school mistake of summarizing and restating what we'd already said earlier. Dr. Canedo would have none of that. Instead, he would ask, "So what?"—as in "So what if you came up with an interesting insight about a particular book or author; why should I care? What makes it important to me or to anyone else?"

Dr. Canedo was right about endings. In really great pieces, the writer not only conveys an important message but makes readers feel as though that message matters to them personally. This isn't easy, but it's worth working for because it makes a huge difference in the impact your writing can have.

TIP:

Keep in mind that readers must expend a certain amount of time and energy to read your work. To do this, they have to give up other things. Instead of reading your piece, for example, they could be watching their favorite TV show, downloading the latest hit songs, or day-trading on the stock market through their parents' brokerage account. Who knows what fun, excitement, and potential profit they have chosen to forego simply to read your writing? As such, they have a right to expect some return on their investment. Specifically, they have a right to ask, "So what? What does this piece have to do with me? Why should I care about it?" And that's exactly the question your ending needs to answer.

Miss Margot says

Remember how I told you I asked, "Why should I care?" at the beginning of every piece? Here's Dr. Canedo telling us to ask that again at the end. That's because you have to keep the "So, what?" in your head through the whole story. Bringing it back at the end in the form of one of the four kinds of endings ensures that people leave your story with something more.

ENDINGS TO AVOID

Some endings are good, some are bad, and some are just plain awful. Having already told you how hard I think endings are, I certainly won't be too grumpy if you occasionally write a bad one. I know I have, probably more than once. That said, however, there are certain endings we should probably all try to avoid:

- **The "The End" ending.** "The End."

  This not a real ending, merely the announcement of one. It's fine for children's stories where your audience might be too young to realize that you're done, but for mature readers, it's a letdown.

- **The "I hope you liked my story" ending.** "Well, that's all I have to say. I hope you liked my story!"

  If I did like the story, this ending would quickly help to change my opinion of it. And if I didn't like it, I doubt I'll like it any better just because the writer hopes I will.

- **The "Tell'em what ya told'em" ending.** "In this paper, I have just discussed blah, blah, blah..."

  I don't know who started this but I sure wish they'd stop. Somewhere, a long time ago, somebody started telling kids their papers should look like this: (Introduction) "Tell 'em what you're gonna tell 'em." (Body) "Tell 'em." (Conclusion) "Tell 'em what ya told 'em." Now, by my count that means you have to write everything three times and your poor reader has to read everything three times. This seems excessive, if not pointless. If you've already told me something, and if I'm any kind of a reader at all, I certainly don't want to hear about it again, let alone two more times.

- **The "It was only a dream" ending.** "I was just about to... when I woke up. It was only a dream."

  I know it's tempting to use this ending when you're writing a long story you don't know how to finish. But readers usually hate it when stories end this way.

TIPS FOR HAPPY ENDINGS

As I've probably mentioned fifty times in this short section, endings are hard. So here are a few tips that I hope will make them easier:

- **Start slow and build.** The first endings we write are usually a single sentence long. That's fine. It's enough just to get the feeling of an ending when you're starting out. After you're comfortable with one-sentence endings, try a one-paragraph ending. This is not as hard as it seems. Just take your one-sentence ending and add a few details to it. Most of the time, I hope you'll be writing fairly short pieces, maybe 500 words or less. In this case, a one-paragraph ending is all you need. When you're working with longer pieces, your ending may become a separate section of several paragraphs.

- **Go long.** Because endings are so hard, most of us don't like to write them. And because most of us don't like to write them, we tend to write them too short. Whenever I read an ending that is too short, I feel like the writer couldn't wait to get finished. I can almost sense the discomfort of someone struggling to eke out a sentence where a full paragraph would be better. It's as though I can feel the writer's anxiety and this makes me feel anxious, too.

- **Write your ending before you get there.** One thing I often do is write my ending ahead of time. I'll get into my piece, maybe a third of the way through, just enough to understand my topic. Then I'll think about where I'm going to go with it and I'll stop to write the ending. Even if it's not perfect—and it usually isn't—I still have something I can work with. Once I have an ending in place, I can go back to wherever I was and head toward the finish line with confidence because I actually know where it is.

- **Remember that the ending is the last thing your audience will read.** As we've talked about before, you have a lot of responsibility when it comes to ending your piece effectively. After all, the ending is the last thing your readers will read, and that means they're likely to remember it better than any other part of your piece. But this means you have an opportunity, too. You can use your ending to say something very important with the knowledge that your readers will be listening closely to your every word. There are only two places where you can count on having your reader's full attention. One is at the beginning, the other is at the end.

Miss Margot says

There's a great device called "book-ending" where writers make their beginning and ending work together like a matched set of bookends. Bookends keep a stack of books together by holding each end in place so the books don't fall over. Book-ending keeps your story together by holding your ideas in place. Ending your story with a reference to how you began keeps your ideas in order and makes a better story with a strong conclusion. Watch how Mr. Peha does it; he uses book-ending in many sections of this book.

WELL, THIS IS CERTAINLY EMBARRASSING

Here we are at the end of our discussion on endings and I'm not sure if I have a good ending for you. I could tell you what I think: endings are hard, but worth the effort to master. I could tell you what I want you to do: study models of good endings. I could tell you how I feel: a little unsure of myself in taking on such a hard topic to write about. Or I could tell you about the future: I hope someday you learn to feel confident about endings because they're such an important part of what we do as writers, and besides, every piece needs one.

Hmmm. Maybe that'll do the trick.

ACTIVITY: CHECKING UP ON MR. PEHA

I think of myself as being pretty good at endings, but am, I, really? Each section of this book is written as a separate short article. There are almost 100 of them and each has its own beginning and ending. What do you think of my endings? What types of endings do I use most often? Am I as good at endings as I think I am?

WHAT MAKES THIS WRITING GOOD?

Sometimes the students I work with really surprise me. Below you'll find a charming piece written by a girl who uses simple language to express simple ideas. But what she ends up with is a piece that succeeds in large part precisely because of its simplicity.

The Daffodil Parade

Boom! The trunk slammed. Bang! The car door slammed as we got out of the van. Buses lined up on the sidewalk. The screeches of the buses were annoying. Screech! Screech! We walked and walked until we found a place to sit for the parade.

I saw a Grease van and someone threw me a daffodil. The petals were soft, it smelled pretty. A Titanic float sailed by. The schools had cheers. One school's band was Star Wars. A dummy was shot out of a cannon. It made me jump. We ate snacks at the parade like sandwiches and juice and carrots. They were good. We sat on a blanket. Things blew everywhere when the floats went by, whew-clunk!

Finally, the parade was done. We put the blanket in the trunk. Boom! It slammed again and we drove away as I thought how much fun I had.

She starts off the piece with sounds. This is an easy and effective lead strategy, especially when you're describing an event with a lot of action. If you've ever been to a parade, you know she's giving you a good sense of what it's like to get settled before it starts.

In the second paragraph, she gives a ton of detail about the day. She talks about the floats, some of the action, what they ate for lunch. At the end of the paragraph, she uses sound again, this time to describe the floats as they go by.

In the last paragraph, she ends her piece with the bookend technique by bringing back the boom and bang of a blanket going in the trunk and the trunk slamming closed. That's pretty sophisticated for such a simple piece.

Now, there are certainly many things that could be added to this short piece to make it better. For example, we don't get as much detail about the parade as we might like, and the detail we do get reads like a list instead of a story. But as simple pieces go, I think it's very successful.

THE RESPECT TO WHICH THEY ARE ENTITLED

I've been a professional writer for about twenty years now, and I've been teaching writing almost as long. I own over 200 books on writing, some of which I've actually read. And yet I can't for the life of me recall any professional writer ever talking about titles. Almost every piece of writing has a title; it's the first thing readers read, but apparently it's not the first thing writers think about.

I guess this means I'm not like most writers because I think about titles all the time. And I hope when I'm done with this short section, you'll be thinking about them, too.

Even as a kid in school, when you couldn't have paid me to write, I got a kick out of coming up with titles. Sometimes the only part of an assignment I'd write would be the title. Clever though I was at coming up with catchy phrases to describe my work, my teachers were often unimpressed: "Hey, Ms. Smith!" I might exclaim. "How 'bout I call my math assignment Fraction Action?" To which Ms. Smith would reply, "How 'bout I call your mother and tell her you're not getting your work done?"

While I wouldn't encourage you to take this titling thing so far that you actually neglect the piece, I want to take a moment in this brief section to make a case for how important titles are and how we should all give some thought, especially when revising, to what the perfect title for a piece might be.

WHY DON'T WRITERS TALK ABOUT TITLES?

Perhaps the reason why writers don't talk about titles is because they are often not the people who write them. Journalists, for example, rarely get to choose the titles of their pieces. Part of the editorial process at a newspaper is having a headline writer put a title on a story after it has been written and edited. And don't think for a minute that the journalist who wrote it gets a say in what the headline is. Once a story is filed, the reporter is done with it, except in cases where fact checking and other verification of details might be required.

The situation isn't that much different in the book world. Editors and publishers are usually the ones who get the final say on titles, although writers can certainly make suggestions. From the standpoint of some-one who is paying to publish something, and hoping to sell a lot of it to make a lot of money, choosing the small string of words that will forever identify the work in the public mind is considered far too important to leave to mere writers.

But most of us don't have big, fancy publishers with lots of money to spend on teams of advertising and marketing wizards who can conjure up the perfect phrase, so we have to do the conjuring up ourselves. And, for my money at least, that's the way it should be. If I write it, I want to decide what to call it.

KINDS OF TITLES

One thing I learned early on, though I have no idea how I learned it, was that there were actually different kinds of titles I could choose from and that part of the fun was thinking of which kind to choose. Here are some I like:

- **Titles that rhyme.** You can probably tell from my little story about "Fraction Action" that I like titles that rhyme. Rhyming titles always sound playful to me. They're good for funny pieces or pieces where you want to poke fun at something serious.

- **Titles that use alliteration.** Alliteration happens when more than one word in a phrase begins with the same sound. The title of the piece "Dolls of Doom" uses alliteration. These are some of my favorite titles. Like the rhyming titles, they often have a playful quality to them.

- **Really short titles.** Some titles are just a single word like the piece, "Chores," for example. Short titles are great because they're easy to remember and often catch the reader by surprise.

- **Really long titles.** Some writers intentionally choose very long titles, such as *From the Mixed Up Files of Mrs. Basil E. Frankweiler.* Like the rhyming and alliteration titles, long titles like this often sound comic. But they can sound mysterious, too, and that's why they're often used for mysteries.

- **Titles with subtitles.** Sometimes writers give us two titles for the price of one. In this case, one is the main title and the other is an extra title that tells more about it. For example, *It Finally Happened at Fenway: How the Red Sox Beat the Yankees and Broke the Curse of the Bambino.* This kind of title is most often used in non-fiction writing. Like a lead, it catches the reader's attention and hints at what the piece is about.

TIP:

Just as with beginnings and endings, there are many different kinds of titles. And just as we can learn new beginnings and endings by studying the writing we enjoy, we can add to our repertoire of titling strategies exactly the same way.

WHY ARE TITLES SO IMPORTANT?

The world is full of print. Every day, hundreds of texts beg us to read them. And most of that begging is done by the title. The title is the part of a piece that jumps off the page and, in a voice that sounds more like a command than an invitation, says, "May I have your attention, please?"

When I'm looking at a pile of newspapers on a table, I read the head-lines first to see if there's anything that interests me. When I flip through a magazine while waiting at the doctor's office, I compare titles in the table of contents to pick the one article I think I'll have time to read. When I scan an article on a web page for important information, I check the title to see if I'm on the right track.

For better or worse, titles are usually the first words readers read. They're big, they're bold, and they give us a hint about whether the piece they belong to will be worth our time. Sadly, most of us don't think too much about writing titles. And nobody ever seems to talk about revising them. But given how important titles are in the readers' experience of a text, I think it makes sense to give them the respect to which they are entitled.

Miss Margot says

On my high school newspaper, hardly anyone wanted to write headlines (what journalists call titles). It was hard. In a paper or magazine, you don't have a lot of space for headlines, so you have to choose your words carefully. I learned a lot about writing by trying to summarize stories in five or six words.

HOW LONG DOES MY PIECE HAVE TO BE?

As we revise a piece over and over, we're inclined to think about its length. When our writing needs a lot of work, it's tempting to just lop off a few big sections and strive for something short and simple. But writing short is far from simple because it forces us to be more accurate in the words we choose and in the ways we use them. Long pieces give us freedom to make mistakes, to have a few parts here and there that aren't exactly perfect. But long pieces often require many hours of revision.

Since teachers have been teaching writing, students have been asking, "How long does my piece have to be?" I know that when I was in school, my friends and I often asked this question. Our intention was to find out how much or how little work we would be expected to do. Usually we got a minimum word count or a minimum number of pages we needed to fill. And then we set about filling them, often with less concern for quality than for length.

This is the problem with the traditional minimum length requirements we get used to in school: when someone tells you to write at least 500 words, or fill at least five pages, or have at least three details, part of the message you're getting is that the amount you write is more important than what you have to say. This is not at all the message I am trying to convey.

So rather than think only about a certain number of words or pages, or even a certain amount of time you should be spending, I'd like you to consider the following:

- **Think function, not form.** When you set out to write a piece of a certain minimum length, you're thinking about what it will look like in its final form: a pile of paper so many pages high with so many words, sentences, or paragraphs. What you're not thinking about is how that pile of paper should function as a piece of written communication. Specifically, you're not thinking about what all those words, sentences, and paragraphs should accomplish in the mind of a reader. In writing, as in many things, form should follow function, not the other way around.

- **Think reader, not writer.** To help me figure out how long a piece should be, I often consider how long a reader will feel like reading it. The average reader reads about 200 words a minute. Most of the time, I'm pretty sure I can capture two to three minutes of someone's time. So that gives me maybe 500 words to work with. If I end up with something 2,000 words long, I know I'll need to keep the reader's attention for ten minutes or more. That might not be so easy. After all, it's not as if I'm working on the next Harry Potter book or something.

- **Think maximum, not minimum.** As is so often the case, the real world is the opposite of school. In school, most teachers will tell you the minimum number of words you can turn in. In the real world, assignments almost always come with a maximum word count. Sometimes this is because we're writing for a newspaper or magazine that has a fixed amount of space to fill. But more often than not, we write to certain lengths because these are the lengths publishers have become accustomed to publishing and readers have become accustomed to reading.

Miss Margot says

I never get the opportunity to write pieces that are as long as I want them to be, or as long as I think the reader wants them to be. That's because in my business we're given a specific amount of space to fill—and that's it! Even if I want to go longer on a story, I know my editors have a pretty good idea of how long our readers will stay on it. They do the thinking, so I don't get to.

BEGINNING, MIDDLE, END, YADDA, YADDA, YADDA

Since kindergarten, you've probably been hearing that a piece of writing has to have a beginning, a middle, and an end. This is true. But once again, this speaks only to the form of a piece, what it should look like. It doesn't say anything at all about what each of these three parts should accomplish, or how you might go about accomplishing it. As such, it's useless information.

When we buy into the traditional "beginning-middle-end" message of school, we once again buy into the idea that form is more important than function, that how your writing looks is more important than what your writing says. To avoid this trap, consider the following:

- **What is the beginning supposed to do?** The beginning of a piece must catch the readers' attention. It has to pull your readers in and pique their curiosity; it has to make them want to read more. Of course, your readers have to have at least some inkling of what they're reading, so you also have to introduce the topic in a successful way. To make sure you have an effective beginning, ask yourself these questions: Will my readers have a hint as to what my piece is about? Will my readers think my piece is going to be worth reading? Will my readers want to find out more?

- **What is the middle supposed to do?** The middle of a piece must deliver on the promise of the beginning. It must clearly convey your main idea with ample, but not excessive, supporting details. It must also answer all of the readers' important questions. To make sure you have an effective middle, ask yourself these questions: Will my readers think I included enough details to help them understand my main idea? Will my readers have enough information so they don't have any important unanswered questions? Will my readers think I included the right amount of information?

- **What is the ending supposed to do?** The ending has to make the piece feel finished and leave your readers with something important to think about. It also has to make your readers feel that the time and energy they devoted to reading your piece was worthwhile. To make sure you have an effective ending, ask yourself these questions: Will my readers feel that my piece is finished? Will my readers feel that my ending gave them something important to think about? Will my readers feel that their time was well spent?

GEE, MR. PEHA. THANKS FOR ALL THAT SWELL INFORMATION, BUT I STILL WANT TO KNOW HOW LONG MY PIECE SHOULD BE

Your piece should be long enough for you to say the most important things you need to say and answer your readers' most important questions—and not one word longer!

CHAPTER FIVE

Be an Editor

TEN THINGS YOU NEED TO KNOW
EVEN IF YOU DON'T READ THIS CHAPTER

1 Editing means something different depending on whether you're working at home, at school, or in the world of professional writing.

2 When editing at school, you should expect some help from your teacher, but your teacher shouldn't do your editing for you.

3 If you ask someone for help with editing, be very specific about the help you need. This is not only respectful, it also increases your odds of getting the help you're looking for.

4 Editing is hard because there's no single official set of rules for writing.

5 Different publishers have their own rules. This is called the publisher's style. When you write for other people, you have to follow their rules.

6 In most writing situations, you'll be better off if, instead of following rules, you follow the meaning of what you write to make sure your readers will understand it.

7 Some people refer to spelling, punctuation, grammar, and usage as "mechanics", but a more accurate term, often used in schools today, is "conventions."

8 Instead of thinking of conventions as rules, think of them as tools for shaping the meaning of what you write.

9 People don't edit by rule; they edit by ear and by eye.

10 You'll probably like editing more, and do it better, if you care a lot about what you're editing. Choosing a good topic to begin with, and wanting to share your writing with others, can change the way you feel about editing.

A THREE-RING CIRCUS

The last three chapters have focused on pre-writing, drafting, and revising. If you've learned about the writing process in school, you'll probably be able to predict with great confidence that this chapter will focus on editing. But that's about all you may be able to predict.

Editing should be the simplest part of the writing process, but in many ways it's the most complicated—or at least the most controversial. Ask a group of people what they think editing is and their answers are likely to be fairly similar; most will probably say things like, "Making corrections", "Fixing little things", or "Preparing a piece for publication". But exactly what these things mean, how they get done, and who ends up having to do them can vary dramatically depending on whether you're writing for yourself at home, writing for your teachers at school, or writing for a publisher in the professional world.

As I was thinking of how I wanted to organize this chapter, it occurred to me that I had a kind of three-ring circus on my hands. All I want to do is tell you a little about editing to help you get started with it, but in order to do that I have to talk about how it works in three different contexts—home, school, and the professional world—all at the same time.

EDITING AT SCHOOL

Editing was a simple matter when I was in school because it never mattered. In all my years as a student, I can't ever remember doing it—not once. Back then, in the Stone Age of the 1970s, I'd turn in a rough draft and Mrs. So-and-So or Mr. Whats-His-Name would whip out their trusty red pens and proudly point out all my mistakes. The idea was that I would dutifully recopy my piece, along with their corrections, and in so doing, I would learn to write correctly.

Instead I learned something else: that I was a poor writer who made a lot of mistakes, that editing was somebody else's responsibility, and that the key to survival in Language Arts was writing really short sentences that never needed punctuation more complicated than a capital letter at the beginning and a period at the end.

Nowadays, in most of the schools where I work, things are a little different. Some teachers still waste red ink giving kids corrections, but most expect their students to find and fix their own errors. Some teachers spare their students the corrections but also spare them any advice about how to get better. Fortunately, a constructive middle ground exists in some Writer's Workshop classrooms where a student can sit down with his teacher and get individual guided instruction during what is often called an "editing conference."

EXAMPLE:

Done well, editing conferences are valuable for both teacher and student. Students not only get help correcting their errors, they get instruction that helps them learn to correct their writing themselves and makes them less likely to make the same mistakes in the future. Teachers also benefit by being able to see how their students think about the editing problems they encounter.

TIP:

If you're in a class with a good writing teacher who offers regular editing conferences, you'll probably get some good help with your editing. You're also likely to learn things that will make you a better editor on your own. If you're in a more traditional classroom where your teacher relies on the red pen and gives you grammar and punctuation exercises all the time, you may need to get help from someone else if you want to get really good at editing your own writing.

EDITING AT HOME

When you're working at home, you'll probably have to edit all by yourself. This can be hard. Every writer makes mistakes and often these errors are hard to spot, especially after you've read your piece over and over about a thousand times. There are also mistakes writers never spot because they don't understand them. Even writers who have written professionally for years don't have every editing issue figured out. I know I certainly don't.

The key to editing on your own is to know what you know and know what you don't. For example, you probably never forget to capitalize the word "I" but you might have trouble knowing which words to capitalize in titles. When it comes to punctuating dialog, you may know to begin a new paragraph each time a new person starts speaking. But what about all the other rules that go with capturing a conversation in print? When you have to be your own editor, fix what you can first and then ask others to help you fix what you can't.

TIP:

The key to getting other people to help you is being specific about the help you need. If you hand a piece of writing to your mom and ask for only general editing help by saying something like, "Will you fix this for me?" or, "Does this look okay?", the response you get is likely to be just as general as the question. But if you're more specific—for example, if you say something like, "Dad, would you help me figure out where my paragraphs go?" —you're much more likely to get your problems solved quickly and thoroughly.

Miss Margot says

When I don't have someone editing for me, I make sure to read everything out loud. I'm always surprised that I find so many errors. But what's really great about reading out loud is that I find problems with fluency, too: where I need a period instead of a comma, where I need to make a new paragraph, or even if I have too many words. We should always read our stuff out loud (even if it's only a whisper), but we *really* should when no one's editing behind us.

EDITING IN THE WORLD OF PROFESSIONAL WRITING

You'd think the worst writers would get the most help with editing. But just the opposite is true. The irony of editing in the world of professional writing is that the best writers get the most help.

Take this book, for example. I'm no slouch as a writer and I'm even a reasonably competent editor. But I get a ton of editing help on this project. In fact, I will actually have two different editors: a development editor and a copy editor.

My development editor will read every draft of every chapter I write and give me ideas for making things better. In general, development editors aren't too concerned with spelling, punctuation, grammar, and usage; they look at larger issues like the ideas writers choose to express and the language they use to express them. Development editors also make sure writers haven't left out anything important or left in things that aren't needed.

After my development editor and I have been through each chapter several times, the writing will go to a copy editor. This is the person who will make sure all my periods and commas are in the right places. This editor also has to make sure the editing conforms to what is called the publisher's style. Every publisher has its own set of rules about how things should be done. It's the copy editor's responsibility to make sure the final manuscript is consistent with these requirements.

Having one person to help with development editing and a second person to do the copy editing is a fairly normal arrangement in professional writing situations. But on really important projects, even more editors may be involved. Sometimes there can be so much editorial help the writer feels like the text is being written by someone else.

Miss Margot says

When I write for magazines, we do what's called "collaborative editing." It's a fancy way of saying that my editor and I work together on the piece to make it better. My editor, Alison points out a lot of stuff that gets by me. She'll tell me when something doesn't make sense and suggest ways of making it clearer. She tells me when she likes something and would like to see more of it. She explains why something doesn't work and offers some solutions for fixing it. She doesn't just mark what's wrong; she helps me make it right. This kind of editing not only makes my articles better; it also makes *me* a better writer.

A DIFFERENT WAY OF THINKING ABOUT EDITING

This brief chapter will not tell you everything you need to know about editing. That would take an entire book. But I do want you to know some important things about it.

Perhaps the most important thing is to understand the challenge of editing. When most people think of editing, they think of fixing a piece of writing so it's perfect. In most cases, this is not possible; language is too complex and the so-called "rules of writing" aren't that consistent. So I'd like you to think about editing a little differently.

Rather than think about editing as something you do to make a piece of writing perfect, I want you to think of it as something you do to make a piece of writing easier and more enjoyable to read. Focusing on readability as opposed to perfection will not only keep you from driving yourself crazy, it'll keep your readers happier, too, because rather than being guided by rules, you'll be guided by the meaning of what you have to say and how you want your audience to hear it.

Editing is complicated and tedious. Few writers enjoy it, and even fewer do it well. As you develop as a writer, you'll undoubtedly get better at editing. But you may never feel that you have mastered it. This means you'll probably always need help from someone to edit every piece you write. Don't worry about this; it's normal. In fact, it's something I recommend. Even though writing is an individual sport, to play our best we need supportive teammates and good coaching.

In school, your teacher should help you, not by correcting your work for you, but by guiding you in the process of learning how to correct it yourself. At home, you can take charge of your editing by asking people for help with specific things you don't yet know how to do.

Then, when you become a successful professional writer and have other professionals to edit for you, you'll be able to take all the energy you used to spend on editing and use it to argue about all the changes editors make to your writing.

Miss Margot says

Some editors ask me to make changes I think are dumb. I used to get really mad and argue with them about it. Now I choose my battles more carefully. Unless I think the change will mislead or misinform the reader, I agree to do it. I don't always think my editors are right, but at the end of the day, some stupid changes are harmless. After years of putting energy into trying to protect my writing from bad editors, I realized that sometimes it's just not worth it. You have to trust your editors and take your personal feelings out of the situation. It's hard to do, and I still get mad sometimes, but that's the way it is when you're a writer.

BE A WRITER LIKE JENNIFER BRETT

Jennifer Brett graduated from the University of North Carolina in 1994 with a degree in journalism. She has worked at several papers including The Augusta Chronicle and The St. Petersburg Times. She currently writes for The Atlanta Journal-Constituion, covering arts, entertainment, and dining.

Q WHAT KIND OF WRITER ARE YOU?

A I am a dining and entertainment writer for *The Atlanta Journal Constitution*, the Southeast's largest newspaper. I write about restaurants, pop stars, actors and actresses, authors, artists, and other performers. I get paid to eat at great restaurants, read books, and go to concerts, plays, parties, movies, and art exhibitions! It's a great job, but a lot of hard work at smaller newspapers led me to this point. I spent years writing about crime, politics, education, business, and other topics before I started my current job.

Q WHY DO YOU WRITE?

A I learn new things and meet fascinating people every day, and my job as a writer gives me the opportunity to share all that interesting information with readers. Even though I write about true events, I try to tell a story each time I write an article for the paper. My stories are full of suspense, humor, true love, broken hearts, outrageous behavior, and surprise endings. The difference between what I do and what fiction writers do is that the characters and events in my stories are real.

Q

WHAT MADE YOU WANT TO BE A WRITER?

A

When I was in eleventh grade, my school chose two AP English students to enter an essay contest. Contestants were supposed to write about patriotism and democracy. I was selected, along with a very smart boy in my class who went to a great college to become an engineer. He spent days researching the topic and wrote an essay with facts about the American Revolution and other important moments in our country's history. He used lots of big words and fancy phrases. I spent about an hour on my essay. I wrote a simple piece about what democracy and patriotism meant to me, without big words or a complicated history lesson. I won! I had always liked writing, but this was the first time I thought I might have enough talent to pursue a career as a writer. (When a local reporter came to my school to write an article about my winning essay for my hometown paper, I thought she had the coolest job in the world). Also, although facts and reporting are crucial to a job as a news-paper writer, this early victory taught me that simple, clear writing can be the best way to communicate with readers.

Q

WHAT ADVICE WOULD YOU GIVE TO A FELLOW WRITER WHO WAS JUST STARTING OUT?

A

Read great newspapers like *The Wall Street Journal*, *The New York Times*, and *The Washington Post*—and mine, of course! Read great magazines like The *New Yorker* and *Harper's*. Read great books, not just the classics. Find contemporary books by gifted writers like the elegantly written *White Oleander* by Janet Fitch. She shows that vivid imagery doesn't have to involve a bunch of five-dollar words and strangled sentences. Ask your English teacher for extra credit, and when you have writing assignments, ask for an honest appraisal of your work. No one gets better on a steady diet of praise.

WHY IS EDITING SO HARD?

Many writers find editing frustrating. We just don't understand why it has to be so hard. Fortunately, one's ability to edit effectively doesn't depend on solving this puzzle. But if you're a curious person like I am—and something of a language geek as well—you might find the answer interesting, so I think I'll take a few minutes of your time and try to explain it.

Why is editing so hard? History.

Editors usually concern themselves with four things: spelling, punctuation, grammar, and usage. They want every word spelled right, every word to mean what it's supposed to mean, and every sentence to follow the rules they are familiar with.

But where do those rules come from? History.

Things would be easier for all of us if the rules came from one source like the Bureau of Official Rules for Editors (BORE). In this scenario, there would be only one official way to do things, and every editor would happily do it that way. To be honest, if things were this straightforward, writers could probably learn the rules themselves and editors wouldn't be needed. But there isn't a single source for every rule; in fact, there are many sources, and they often conflict with each other.

Why are there so many conflicting sources? History.

A NOT ENTIRELY COMPLETE HISTORY OF THE RULES OF WRITING

People started "writing" with pictures about 5,000 years ago. About 2,500 years later, they started using letters. For a few hundred years they didn't have vowels, but apparently no one was bothered by this. Eventually, things got worked out and we ended up with the 26 letters we have today. I like to think that having all those letters made writers so happy they forgot about everything else, including periods, capitals, commas, and even spaces because

THEFIRSTWRITINGPEOPLEDIDWITHLETTERSLOOKEDLIKETHIS

It was called *scripto continuo,* or "continuous writing." This saved writers a lot of effort, and certainly made editors unnecessary, but readers weren't exactly thrilled. Over the next 1,000 years or so, writers started putting their own marks all over their work to make it easier to read. This helped a little, but things still weren't right because writers used different marks to mean the same thing and everyone was spelling words more or less any way they wanted.

Then, in the 15th century, a guy named Johann Gutenberg invented a machine that could print books. His machine required many little pieces of wood or metal shaped like letters and marks of punctuation. Printers and publishers quickly got tired of creating special shapes to support every writer's individual way of punctuating, so they began to standardize the shapes they would use. Of course there were many different publishers and no Bureau of Official Rules for Editors to bore them into submission, so even though punctuation marks, spelling, and other rule-related aspects of writing were being standardized to some degree, they weren't being standardized completely for everyone.

With each passing century, the rules of writing have become more consistent. But there is still no official way of doing everything. Each publisher has its own set of rules and these rules are referred to as the publisher's style. The rules are usually written down and published in a style guide. However, even though this guide sets forth the rules editors should follow, situations arise all the time that are not accounted for, so new rules have to be invented on the spot. Language simply changes too quickly and is too complex to be described in a set of permanent rules we could all learn and use forever.

HOW WE GOT STANDARD SPELLING

In the United States, during the early part of the nineteenth century, a man named Noah Webster put us on the path to standardized spelling by creating the first comprehensive collection of American English words. His method was simple and sensible: look at how certain words were being spelled, look for patterns among similarly-spelled groups of words, and make judgments about which spellings seemed most logical. But American English was already 200 years old. It was constantly acquiring words from other languages at such a rate not even Webster could make American spelling logical enough. He could, however, standardize American spelling by publishing his work, which became so popular many homes in America at that time had only two books: the *Bible* and *Webster's Dictionary*.

Over the next 150 years or so, the spelling of English words settled into something regular and now we have spellcheckers in our computers that can tell us—most of the time—when we've made a mistake. This doesn't mean you don't have to learn to spell. It merely means that when you write with a computer, you can get a little help to make sure your spelling is accurate.

Miss Margot says

Spellcheckers may act like your friend, but if you're not careful, they can end up being your enemy. That's because spellcheckers only catch words that aren't in their dictionaries. So if you meant to use "to" to write, "I'm going to school", but you typed t-o-o, your spellchecker wouldn't register that as a mistake. On the flip side, if you use a word like my name, Margot, your spellchecker will tell you it's misspelled, even though it's not. So, spellcheckers can help, but you should always proofread carefully and get help with words you're not sure about.

Even though every word has a correct or official spelling now, this doesn't mean everyone can be a perfect speller. While most people can remember the correct spelling of most of the words they use regularly, some people struggle with this. But problems with spelling do not affect, and are not related to, a person's ability to think clearly and write well. So if you're not a good speller, you can still be a sharp thinker and a great writer. You'll just have to work a little harder to get your spelling corrected, either by using a computer or asking someone for help.

WHY WE DON'T HAVE STANDARD GRAMMAR AND USAGE

Around the same time Noah Webster became interested in standardizing spelling, others became interested in standardizing the way people spoke and wrote. These people were interested in grammar—the way we put words together to make sentences. Most of these people were wealthy and had been educated in Europe. Because of their background, they wanted the rules of American English to be based in part on the rules of Latin. Problem was, nobody spoke Latin anymore; it died out with the Roman Empire over a thousand years before.

This created an interesting situation as a wealthy and powerful class of people educated in Europe tried to get everyone in America to speak in a way they probably couldn't learn unless they had been born into a wealthy and powerful class of people educated in Europe. And speaking was only part of the issue because these people wanted the rules of writing to match the rules of speech as well. If you've ever spoken to anyone in our country, you know there's a problem with the idea that everyone should speak the same way: everyone speaks differently because we all grow up in different kinds of families. Learning to use grammar that is different from the grammar your family uses can be extremely challenging. And this is why people argue so much about grammar and usage: one group of people wants something very badly that it can probably never have.

Today this battle rages on all over America. On one side are people called *prescriptivists*. They want to prescribe how people in America should communicate. Prescriptivists believe in clear right and wrong rules about speaking and writing; they want everyone to speak and write the same way. Then there are the *descriptivists*. These people like to study how different people communicate and describe what they observe. They tend not to believe in simple right or wrong answers when it comes to issues of grammar and usage, preferring instead to put their energy into understanding different styles of communicating as opposed to declaring which one is best for all of us to use.

WHY WE'LL ALWAYS BE ARGUING ABOUT STANDARD PUNCTUATION

Issues of spelling are pretty much settled these days, and even though people argue about grammar and usage, those arguments can often be resolved by referring to some kind of reference book. Yet some aspects of punctuation—particularly the use of commas—still give us headaches and, once again, history is to blame.

The problem is that for almost 2,000 years, three different traditions of punctuation have competed against each other and, as a result, things haven't been quite as consistent as most people would like. In the past, some people wanted to punctuate writing so it could be read out loud in certain rhythms and with dramatic starts and stops. Other people wanted sentences punctuated strictly according to rules of grammar. All the while, or at least since Gutenberg's time, printers wanted rules that would suit the mechanical nature of their work.

What this means is that if you hold up a newspaper, a web page, and a book side by side, you're likely to see some differences in how things are punctuated. And, personally, I don't think this will ever change. I simply can't imagine a world where everyone agrees to punctuate the same way.

Miss Margot says

Even people in journalism can't agree on punctuation. There are two kinds of people in journalism: those who follow AP Style and those who follow Chicago Style. I can tell right away who follows which style just by reading a paragraph of their writing. Because Mr. Peha and I follow different styles, we're always playing this game of moving commas around. Actually, I have no idea what style Mr. Peha follows and I don't think he knows either. Mr. Peha says, "I don't follow a style; I follow the meaning of what I write to make sure it's as clear as possible to my readers." But one thing we do agree on is that when you *do* use a comma, it should make the meaning of the sentence clearer.

SO WHAT'S A POOR WRITER TO DO?

Remember what I said a while back about following the needs of your readers? That's the key to sorting all this out. Regardless of how someone decides to write something, someone else has to read it. And this is what writers should think about when they think about spelling, punctuation, grammar, and usage.

Donald Murray, a Pulitzer Prize-winning writer and one of the best writing coaches in the country, once said, "The writer should not follow rules but follow language toward meaning."

Every time you make a decision about where to put a comma or how to style a sentence, re-read what you've written and follow the trail of language you've created to the meaning your reader will discover in the end. If the meaning expressed isn't what you intended, try something else. You can read a hundred writing rule books, but none of them will be more effective than simply reading your own work and asking the question, "What will my reader think?"

WHAT MAKES THIS WRITING GOOD?

When I was a kid in school, I thought a piece of writing had to be long to be good. But now I know different. Take a look at this little gem below. It's less than 150 words, but I'd challenge anyone who says it isn't a complete piece of writing.

The Last Day of School

I sat in my desk, sweat dripping down my face. I shut my eyes tight, then opened them. I looked at my watch: 11:27. Three minutes! Three minutes until I heard a sound, a sound that would set me free for three months of total nothingness. Ms. Smith rambled on about pi and figuring out percentages. 11:28. I stared at my watch. I looked as the seconds ticked down to freedom from school. 11:29:50. 10, 9, 8, 7, 6, 5, 4, 3, 2, 1, 0 BRRRIIINNNGGG! The bell rang. I pulled on my backpack, tore out of the room, sprinted down the stairs, sped down the hallway, and bounded out the door. I dashed home and picked up a snack. I popped a video into the VCR, turned on the TV, and relaxed. Ah, what a glorious day!

There are several things in this piece (like a teacher teaching a math lesson during the last three minutes of the school year) that lead me to believe it's not entirely true. But it's so good I just don't care.

Instead of capturing the truth of the last few minutes of the year, I think this writer is trying to capture the feeling. And I think he does it perfectly.

One thing that strikes me immediately about this piece is how good the sentences are. The writer does a great job of showing us the energetic feeling of the scene by giving us so many short sentences. But every once in a while, he works in a long one. This adds variety and suspense; we can't wait to find out what happens next.

Part of the writer's success with sentences comes from the fact that this piece is so well edited. Look at all the different conventions the writer has to deal with. As I read it, there are no mistakes (though some editors may take exception to this).

Perhaps best of all is the pacing, the way the story speeds up and slows down as it goes along. The story starts out slow and builds beautifully up to the moment when the bell rings. Then, just as we can imagine the kids tearing out of the room, the writer pulls us along with him as he begins a long sentence that gets him out of his seat and out the door. Two sentences later, he's got a snack to eat and a movie to watch. As we reach the end, we share the writer's satisfaction. Ah, what a glorious story!

THINK TOOLS, NOT RULES

When I was in school, the term we used for spelling, punctuation, grammar, and usage was "mechanics", but today you might find your teachers calling these things "conventions." This is probably a better word. First of all, there's nothing very mechanical about figuring out where a comma goes. It's hard work and every bit as creative at times as any other part of writing. But more importantly, the term "conventions" is more accurate because it refers to the idea that our writing looks the way it does because we've all just gotten used to it looking that way. There is such a thing as "conventional" writing (the writing we're used to) even if there isn't a single book of rules somewhere that describes it perfectly.

Writers use conventions to enhance and clarify the meaning of what they write. For example, a capital letter at the start of a sentence tells us a new idea is beginning; a period at the end tells us the idea is finished. Conventions allow writers to specify the exact way a word or phrase should be interpreted and help readers understand exactly what the writer had in mind.

TIP:

Many people, when they think about conventions, think about rules. But as we've already discussed, that's not exactly right. Conventions aren't rules, they're tools for shaping meaning. They help us hammer out a precise idea, nail down a topic, and chisel away at parts of a piece that might mean one thing to us and something different to someone else.

WHAT IS THIS THING CALLED CONVENTIONS?

Famous songwriter Cole Porter probably wasn't thinking too much about the importance of conventions when he whipped up a little number in 1929, called *What Is This Thing Called Love?* But that doesn't mean we can't do a little of the thinking for him. One of the most successful songwriters of his day, Porter wrote dozens of hit songs. How many more could he have written if he used some "conventional" wisdom?

What? Is this thing called love?

What *is* this thing called, love?

What is *this* thing called, love?

What is this *thing* called, love?

"What is this thing?" called Love.

"What is this?" Thing called. "Love?"

"What? Is this Thing?" called Love.

"What is," this thing called, "love?"

"What? Is this," Thing called, "love?"

"What is this thing? Call Ed, love"

As you can see, one simple sentence can be interpreted ten different ways just by rearranging a little punctuation. Some of these sentences make more sense to us than others. And it wouldn't be hard to rearrange things even more to come up with sentences that didn't make any sense at all. For the most part, readers have trouble understanding things when writers present them with arrangements of words and markings they aren't used to. So, again, knowing your readers, and reading your writing with them in mind, is the key to success with conventions.

ACTIVITY: APPLY YOUR OWN CONVENTIONAL WISDOM

You don't have to be a famous songwriter to try your hand at shaping the meaning of a sentence with conventions. It's fun and it's a great way to learn about how conventions work. Almost any short sentence will do. Or take something famous. For example, I took the first line of Herman Melville's *Moby Dick*: "Call me Ishmael." With just three extra question marks, I turned it into a sentence about someone getting a phone call from their friend: "Call? Me? Ishmael?"

HOW DO PEOPLE REALLY EDIT?

Have you ever asked adult writers how they edit their writing? Fortunately you've got one right here. Even though I've got a couple of other editors watching over me on this project, I don't deliver my work to the next person without editing it myself first. And what does that look like? I read my writing over, sentence by sentence, until everything seems right to me. And then I read it over again. Re-reading plays a big part in how everyone edits. But what do people do during all that re-reading?

Most of us who have been doing this for many years edit our writing according to how it sounds when we read it and how it conforms to a few general principles we try to follow. That last sentence is a perfect example. After I wrote it, I thought, "Wow, that's a long sentence. I wonder if I need some commas in there?" (Note the general principle that long sentences often need commas.) I thought about putting a comma after the word "years" because I felt myself take a little pause there. But after reading the sentence again, I realized that a comma there would actually make the sentence harder to read, so I left it out. I also considered putting a comma after "how it sounds when we read it" but again, after re-reading, I realized I didn't need that one either. So now I've got a really long sentence with no commas in it, and because that's a very unusual thing in my experience, I'll read it over one more time to make sure it's okay.

In the process of editing that sentence, I started with my sense of where the idea began and ended. Then I asked myself if I needed any help in the middle to make it easier to read and understand. Any time a sentence of mine is that long, an alarm goes off in my head and I go back to check for commas. Nine times out of ten, with a sentence like this, I'd need at least one or two. But in this case, I didn't. I wasn't looking for a certain number of commas to put in, or a rule that says I have to have one here or there. I was looking to see if putting in a comma or two would make a long sentence easier to read and understand.

TIP:

In school I was always told I had to learn the rules of correct writing in order to write correctly. But in my experience as a writer, this hasn't been true. Most writers I've known, myself included, edit not by rule, but by ear and by eye. We read our writing, sentence by sentence, listening carefully to the voice inside our head. Reading slowly and expressively, we pay close attention to places that might require marks of punctuation, or places where marks already exist. By matching what we hear with what we see—or don't see—we get a sense of what we might want to do. Much of the time, we don't get the right answer right away. At least I don't. Instead, I get a feeling for what the answer might be, just like I did when I tried to figure out if I needed commas in that long sentence.

Figuring out what marks go where is often a process of elimination. For example, I know I'm not going to need any question marks or periods in the middle of a sentence (unless I'm punctuating dialog, and that's another story entirely). I also know that commas are much more common than colons, semicolons, or dasheswhen I'm trying to break a big sentence into small parts. Knowing which marks I'm likely to need in a given situation makes picking the right ones easier.

Often, the best thing I can do is just try out an idea and look at it. For example, here's that long sentence again with the first comma in it after "years":

Most of us who have been doing this for many years, edit our writing according to how it sounds when we read it and how it conforms to a few general principles we try to follow.

This doesn't seem right to me. The word "edit" is the action in the sentence and the phrase, "Most of us who have been doing this for many years" represents the people who are doing the editing. Putting a comma between them would be like putting a comma in this sentence: "We, edit our writing according to how it sounds when we read it." That would be silly. Sometimes I use this kind of substitution technique to find out how a sentence works and to determine how best to punctuate it.

Even the best professional editors sometimes use trial and error approaches like this. I hope they're a little faster at it than I am, not to mention more accurate.

We're all taught that writing correctly is about following rules. And I don't want to give you the impression that there aren't rules to follow. There are rules, and some people get very angry when we neglect them. But nobody I know actually uses rules when they edit. And nobody I know ever learned to edit well by memorizing rules. Writers learn to edit well by learning to read well and to think well.

LEARNING TO LIKE EDITING

I was going to call this section, "Learning to Love Editing" but I figured that was going too far. It's hard for me to imagine anyone truly loving editing. But I do believe there are people who like it, and I'm convinced that learning to like it can make us better at it.

There's no doubt about it; editing is hard work. And yet, I think everyone knows how important it is to write correctly. We live in a very judgmental culture, and even when readers find just a few errors in a piece of writing, they tend to judge the writer as lazy, unintelligent, or both. This isn't necessarily true, and it certainly isn't fair, but it does happen and we all need to be aware of it.

173

I think I told you already about my experience with editing in school. I just didn't see why my teachers spent all that time fussing over little things that didn't seem to make much of a difference. The fact that I was bad at editing probably had something to do with how I felt about it, too. So I just decided to avoid it. I only used words I knew how to spell. I wrote short sentences so I wouldn't have to worry about commas. I never used dialog because I could tell from reading it how complicated the punctuation was. And everything I wrote was as short as I could get away with, so that when I did make mistakes at least I'd make as few as possible.

Then one day everything changed. I was in college taking a course I was really interested in from a professor I really liked. My first paper was due, and I wanted to do well on it. For the first time in my life, I cared about my writing, and more importantly, I cared what other people thought about it, too. All of a sudden, my editing started to improve and so did my feelings about it.

TIP:

Editing takes effort. And the amount of effort writers put into it is roughly equal to how much they care about what they're writing and who they're writing for. Because of this, the first step in producing correct writing may not have anything to do with correctness at all. Instead, it may have to do with picking a topic you're interested in, writing for people you care about, and thinking about how you will appear to them as they read what you've written.

TEN TIPS FOR BETTER EDITING

You may have caught on by now that I won't be going over every mark of punctuation, every rule of grammar, or every suggestion for proper usage. You'd be holding a phone book in your hand if I did. But I don't feel right sending you out into the cold, cruel world of editing without a few specific tips. So here goes:

1 **Get your word's worth.** It's so easy to lose a word, especially a little one like "the" or "and." Before you get too far trying to figure out commas and semicolons, make sure your writing includes all the words it's supposed to have. Looking for words that are missing, duplicated, or just plain wrong should be the first thing on your editing checklist.

2 **Lock down your sentences.** Once you know all the words are there, make sure you can find the beginning and end of each sentence. The sentence is the basic unit of meaning in a piece. It's also the basic unit of punctuation. It makes no sense trying to solve problems on the insides of your sentences if you don't know where the outsides are.

3 **Draft with block paragraphing.** Most people are aware that there are two ways to indicate a paragraph: by indenting and by skipping a line. Your editing will be easier if you use the skip-a-line, or "block" style when you draft. This makes it easier to see where paragraphs begin and end. You can switch to indented paragraphs when you get ready to publish.

4 **When it comes to commas, if in doubt, leave them out.** There has been a general trend over the last fifty years to use less punctuation. This is especially true of commas. So if you're wondering about whether to add one here or there, odds are you'll be better off if you don't.

5 **Make sure you can see what you're doing.** Many editing errors occur only because the editor didn't see them. When working on the computer, use a font like Verdana that has been designed for optimal readability rather than the typical Times, Arial, or Helvetica, which are very hard to read on screen. If you're working with pen and paper, printed handwriting is usually easier to read than cursive.

6 **Come back later.** The best advice you'll ever get about editing is to read and re-read. Unfortunately, this can also be the worst advice as well. Reading over the same passage too many times can cause you to ignore simple problems. To make sure this doesn't happen, put the piece down for as long as you can and then go back over it again when you're fresh.

7 **Try it out loud.** Hardly anybody does this, but it really does work. You'll pay closer attention to the details of your writing if you read it out loud. I've caught many errors in my own writing this way. Sometimes, if I'm trying to fix a particularly complex sentence, reading it out loud is the only way I can do it.

8 **Editing dialog? Grab a novel.** Punctuating dialog is the most complex editing task there is. Even on my best days, I find it hard to keep all the rules straight. That's when I grab a novel and see how someone else does it. Just turn to a part where people are talking and you'll have all the information you need.

9 **Finish your revising first.** This has happened to me more than once: I spend half an hour editing a passage to perfection only to discover that I need to rewrite it later. It's okay to edit lightly here and there at any stage of the writing process. But save your heavy duty editing until after you know you're done revising.

10   **Use the "extra" comma at the end of a list.** My wife and every other journalist in the country will hate me for this, but I think it's always better to put in that last comma in a list. There's no penalty for including it and it always makes your writing easier to read: "My favorite kinds of music are rap, rock and roll and hip hop." or "My favorite kinds of music are rap, rock and roll, and hip hop."

So, are you prepared for every editing situation you'll ever encounter? Hardly. But then, nobody ever is. I've been editing my own writing for over twenty years and I still struggle with it almost every time I prepare my own pieces for publication. I also find, to my horror and amazement, that even after putting in hours editing a piece to perfection, it still isn't perfect. I honestly don't think I've ever turned in perfect work in my life. Even more sobering is the fact that I don't know if I'm any better now than I was when I finished college.

There is one thing I have improved and that's my knowledge of myself as a writer. I know most of my bad habits at this point and that helps me keep them in check. I've also learned an interesting thing about those times when I just can't figure out how to make something work. If I catch myself editing a sentence or two over and over and I just can't figure out some aspect of the punctuation or grammar, I almost always come to realize that I simply didn't know what I wanted to say. It turns out that for me, the best editing advice is to be clear about what I'm trying to write. Once my ideas are in good shape, my editing seems to shape up, too.

CHAPTER SIX

Be a Publisher

TEN THINGS YOU NEED TO KNOW
EVEN IF YOU DON'T READ THIS CHAPTER

1 Publishing, for young writers, is a new thing. A generation ago, hardly anyone ever thought about it.

2 Publishing your writing is a great thing to do. Every young writer should experience it in some way.

3 Computer technology and the growth of the Internet makes it possible for all writers to be their own publishers.

4 Publishing our writing changes the way we think about it and helps us take our work more seriously.

5 To publish a piece of writing means to make it available to the public in some way.

6 Writing does not have to be perfect to be published. Writers just have to do everything they know how to do to make their writing as good as it can be.

7 Even though it's very time consuming, and most people don't like to do it, publishing writing by hand often produces a result readers like better than writing published by computer.

8 The writing you publish using a computer will turn out better if you learn a little about formatting, typography, and pagination.

9 Of all the new ways to publish, blogging is by far the most popular. It's cheap, easy, and fast. Just about anyone can set up their own blog in ten minutes.

10 Working on a school newspaper is one of the best publishing experiences a young writer can have.

HOW QUICKLY THINGS CHANGE

As I sat down to begin this chapter, I realized it never would have existed a generation ago when I was in school. In the early 1980s, when I finished high school, the idea of kids publishing their writing wouldn't have made any sense. Kids didn't publish when I was a kid— not for real, or for fun. So what changed?

ATTITUDES CHANGED

In the twenty-five years since I graduated from high school, the teaching of writing has undergone more changes than at any other time in history. Teachers now want kids to write a lot more than they used to and they want them to write differently, too.

Back in my day, even at the high school level, I can remember writing only two or three "papers" a semester. These were formal research-type projects or big assignments in Language Arts based on a book we all read in class. We didn't have much choice in our topics or even in what we got to say about the topics our teachers chose for us. We didn't write much about our own lives or our personal feelings. The teacher was our only audience. And the only purpose we had for writing was to get a grade.

Our teachers didn't think of us as writers back then, and we didn't think of ourselves as writers either. I did have a couple of friends who wrote a lot outside of school, but that work was always separate from anything they did in class; it never would have occurred to them to share it with a teacher because the writing we did in school was so different.

Back then, kids weren't writers, they were just students, and only a few were expected to ever learn to write well. Today, more teachers take the attitude that all kids are writers from the moment they pick up a pencil in kindergarten, and that every one of them can learn to write well if they have good instruction. So if kids are writers, and writers get published, kids have to experience some form of publishing, too. Not every teacher believes this, of course; there are still many traditionalists out there. But enough teachers do that you should definitely have opportunities throughout your school life to publish writing that is meaningful to you.

GOALS CHANGED

The goals we used to have for students in writing also changed. In the past, the only thing teachers seemed to care about was whether their students could write correctly. What they had to say in their writing didn't matter much. Most of the time, our teachers pretty much told us what to write by giving us all the same narrow topics, telling us what structure to use, and making sure all of our papers were the same length. There wasn't a lot of room for individuality.

Nowadays, correct writing is still important, but more teachers are learning to look beyond correctness to the quality of what kids communicate in their work. We want you to have your own ideas and to think them through carefully for yourself. We want what you write about to be meaningful to you and to your audience. We want your writing to sound like nobody else in the world but you could have written it.

Perhaps the most important goal we have now is that we want you to take ownership of your writing. This means we want you to be responsible for every aspect of your work all the way from pre-writing to publishing. Publishing is especially important for helping you develop your sense of ownership because this is where writers concentrate on producing a finished product and on getting it out to their readers.

VALUES CHANGED

Our society's values about writing have changed, too. Writing is now more important than it used to be. College professors want better writing from their students. Employers want employees to write well on the job. The essays you write to get into college carry more weight than they used to. And almost every state in the country makes students take written essay tests at certain grades.

All of a sudden, it seems like everyone cares about writing. So it's only natural that we would want you to care about it, too. One of the best ways to do that is to help you publish. Publishing, even when we do it ourselves, helps us develop a sense of accomplishment about our work. I can't tell you how many times I've watched kids in classrooms go back through all the published pieces they've created during a school year. Sitting there in May, holding 15–20 pieces in your hands and realizing "Hey, I really wrote this!" can be a powerful experience.

TECHNOLOGY CHANGED

Perhaps the biggest change of all has been in technology. As a high school student, the most sophisticated technology I used for writing was an electric typewriter—and I didn't even own one of those; it was locked up in the typing lab. We all wrote with pencil or pen. Publishing our writing, if we wanted to make something like a news-letter, for example, meant writing things out, typing them up, using a photocopier, cutting our work into pieces, and gluing everything in place. It took forever, often looked horrible, and made quite a mess.

Now even young kids can use desktop publishing software on a com-puter. And if you want to skip printing on paper entirely, you can publish your writing on the Internet. You also have many more choices of how your published writing looks. You can choose fonts, change margins, use graphics, pick colors—there's no end to what you can do when you're your own publisher.

ARE YOU READY TO CHANGE?

Reading this book is about changing the way you see yourself. My hope, of course, is that you come to see yourself as a writer. But I also want you to see yourself as a publisher of writing, someone who puts writing out into the world for other people to read and enjoy.

Even if you've written for years, you may not feel this way about yourself. I know I certainly didn't, even in my twenties when I began writing professionally. But something changed in me as the years went by and I think it had to do with publishing. When the Internet caught fire in the 1990s, something inside of me caught fire, too. For the first time, I saw the possibility of being my own publisher. With a simple website, I could feel like I was reaching the world with my words.

This was exciting stuff, and it still excites me today. Even if I'm not a "real" publisher, even if I don't put out books or magazines or newspapers, I can still publish. This means I'm in charge of who reads my writing and how it looks to them when they read it.

The idea of publishing changed me as a writer. It made me work harder and made me take my work more seriously. It also improved the way I felt about editing, which I began to see less as a chore and more as an opportunity. Now I think of everything I write as something that will, in one way or another, be published. And that has changed how I work for the better. Who knows? Publishing might change you, too.

BE A WRITER LIKE KELVIN DE'MARCUS ALLEN

Kelvin De'Marcus Allen is a columnist and public relations consultant. His columns have appeared in The New Haven Register, The News & Observer *(Raleigh, N.C.), and* The Network Journal *(Brooklyn, New York). He is the author of* Looking Back to Move Forward: Reconciling the Past—Liberating the Future.

Q WHAT KIND OF WRITER ARE YOU?

A I'm a columnist. Columnists tend to have a lot of creative freedom and can write about a lot of different topics. A column varies in length, but more often than not it's between 600–1200 words long. I write about my past a lot and I try to tie in some current event or circumstance that a lot of people can relate to. I think most of us are more alike than we are different, and sometimes we need to be reminded of that. If I can get that through in my writing, then I think I've served others well, and that is what is most important to me.

Q WHY DO YOU WRITE?

A To me, writing is like being a musician. Words can be rhythmic, and I enjoy arranging and rearranging words and sentences to catch the reader's attention. And, just like a musician who practices a lot, the more I write, the better I get.

Q

WHAT MADE YOU WANT TO BE A WRITER?

A

I really can't point to one particular incident that inspired me to become a writer. All I know is that I've always enjoyed reading, and I also enjoy learning new words and their meanings. Most of my early writings were never written with the intention of ever sharing them with anyone.

At a very early age I would write down my thoughts about all kinds of things, and that's what really got me going. My older brother, Ronald was a prolific writer and I enjoyed reading his poetry. I suppose deep down inside I felt that if I could ever write half as well as he could, perhaps someone would care to read my writing one day and would enjoy it as much as I enjoyed reading his poetry.

Q

WHAT ADVICE WOULD YOU GIVE TO A FELLOW WRITER WHO WAS JUST STARTING OUT?

A

Read! I've noticed that many young writers don't place much value on reading as it relates to their writing. In my opinion, reading is probably the single most important thing they can do to improve their writing besides making sure that they write something as often as time permits. Another bit of advice that I think is important, particularly if your writing genre is going to be non-fiction, is to be honest. Honesty separates the great writers from the mediocre writers. Words have a way of responding to honesty, and besides I've never met an honest writer who suffered from "writer's block."

WHAT IS PUBLISHING?

As teachers and kids have gotten more interested in publishing, and new technology has made new kinds of publishing possible, I'm often bombarded by questions about it when I give writing workshops: How do I get myself published? What's the best way to publish on my own? What does "publishing" really mean? Does my writing have to be perfect to be published? And so on.

The fact that so many people have so many questions is a good indication of their interest. But I know, too, that all the confusion surrounding publishing sometimes keeps people from pursuing it. And that's not good. So I'll try to clear things up here as best I can.

WHAT DOES "PUBLISHING" REALLY MEAN?

Remember in the last chapter when I was talking about editing and I said I had a three-ring circus on my hands? I've got the same challenge here with publishing. Publishing means different things to different people under different circumstances. Here's what it looks like at school, at home, and in the world of professional writing:

- **Publishing at school.** In school, publishing is the final stage of the writing process. Saying that a piece of writing is published is the same as saying that it's finished. Different teachers have different standards about what a published piece should be. Mostly, this has to do with how much editing is required and who will do it. Some teachers want everything to be perfect. To get it that way, they often end up doing the final editing themselves. That doesn't make much sense to me since editing for students doesn't help them get better. When I teach, my standard is that in order for a piece to be published, a writer has to have done everything he or she knows how to do to make that piece the best it can be. Why do I choose this standard? Because it's exactly the same standard my publishers hold me to as a professional writer.

- **Publishing at home.** At home, you're the publisher. This means that as soon as you think the piece is ready to be read by other people, it's published. Of course, this depends to some extent on who we mean by "other people". If you're just showing it to your mom and dad to see if they like it, that might not feel like publishing. But if you print out fifty copies and give them to your friends, or if you e-mail a story to 100 people, or if you post something on your own website, then you're definitely publishing. When you're the publisher, you set the standard.

- **Publishing in the world of professional writing.** In the traditional sense, a piece of writing is not published until someone else publishes it for you. Take this book, for example. Technically, it won't be published until my publisher releases bound copies for review or sale. Months could go by from the time I finish it to the time it's released, and during this time no one will really see it. Until copies come back from the printer and are delivered to people or bookstores by mail, I won't be able to say it's truly published. When you work with a publisher, the time and manner of publishing is up to them. My publishers don't even have to make books. They could release my writing on a website, CD-ROM, or any other medium they choose. They could also choose not to release it. And then I'd have to look for another publisher or consider publishing the book myself.

Perhaps the best way to understand the concept of publishing is to think of the literal meaning of the word as it relates to our situation. The word "publish" comes from the same Latin root as the word "public". And this, I think, is where the true meaning of the term can be found. To publish your writing is to release it to the public.

THE LINE BETWEEN PUBLIC AND PRIVATE

Writing is a private activity. Even when we do it as one of many writers in a crowded classroom, no one stares at our paper and reads our words. Most teachers I know will even respect students' occasional requests to not have anyone read their writing—even the teacher. So as you write, you're in control of how public your writing is.

At some point, however, most of us start thinking about an audience, and this is where we start to draw the line between public and private. Much of the time, we don't even have to wait until a piece is written; our sense of an audience can materialize at the beginning when we're thinking of something to write about. After all, whether or not a topic is good depends partly on whether or not other people find it interesting.

Once an audience enters the picture, the possibility that someone might read our work becomes real. At this point, it's natural to think about how and when that might happen, and before we know it, we're thinking about publishing. Early on, while we're still writing, we're in control of who reads our work. Even after it's done, we might still only show it to a select group of readers. True publishing happens only when we let it.

EXAMPLE:

What Makes This Writing Good?

There's a feeling many people have, I think, that in order for a piece of writing to be good it has to be filled with big ideas, fancy words, and long complicated sentences. But years of working with young writers have taught me that me this isn't necessarily so. Here's a very successful piece that captures an experience just perfectly using very simple language.

$\Rightarrow$

Ashes All Over

The day after Thanksgiving my family had a reunion for my grand-mother on a boat because she died of cancer about a month ago. We were all sitting in a circle, reading letters about her and saying memories. Then from oldest to youngest we went outside and threw a rose and a cup of grandmother's ashes out into the water. I asked if I could go alone so I could have a special time with grandmother.

When it was my turn, I went outside, said a few words, and threw the rose. Then I picked up the cup and filled it with ashes. But I threw the ashes a little crooked and they fell on the bumpers and because the wind was very hard the ashes blew back all over me and the boat.

Everyone inside was laughing really hard, I was even laughing myself! I thought it was because of what happened. But then my mom told me that she did the same thing to my grandfather four years ago. She said that she twisted her hand a little and the ashes flew back all over her and my Aunt Lilly. That made me laugh even harder, and my mom said Grandma always liked a good laugh.

A little bit later, I got to have the extra roses to throw outside and say what I wanted to say. I thought I would be sad but I wasn't. It was really a wonderful time.

I don't know how you feel about this, but funerals and other kinds of memorial services always make me a bit uncomfortable. But I'm not uncomfortable at all about this story. I think that has to do with the simple way it is told. There's a goal some writers have of telling a true life story without adding anything to it that wasn't really there.

Perhaps the most important quality in a piece of writing is what we call the writer's voice. Voice is hard to describe. Sometimes people call it tone or style, but I think of it more as personality. When a writer's voice is strong, we get a sense of the person behind the words. That is, we feel as though we're getting to know the writer as a person, just as we might if we were hanging out together.

I love the voice in this piece. The whole thing seems true to the way I think an young girl would handle herself in this kind of situation—with a little bit of awkwardness, but also with honesty, humor, and openness to whatever might come up.

PUBLISHING BY HAND

As I type these words into my word processor, I feel odd saying I wish more kids published more writing by hand. In school, of course, the students I work with can't wait to get on the computer. I can certainly understand their impatience because I once felt it, too. But having worked with kids in classrooms for more than ten years, I can honestly say that the published pieces I've enjoyed most have been those that were published by hand.

Every writer's handwriting is a little different and this makes each piece seem more personal and unique to the writer who wrote it. I also love the illustrations and cover pages kids create. Seeing a bunch of students publishing by hand gives a classroom a feel of craftsmanship, and that's a feeling I like to encourage whenever I can.

I recognize that publishing by hand is very hard, especially on long pieces. So, when I'm working with kids who can type, I don't require them to do it very often. But I do encourage them to try. Sadly, the only incentive I can offer is the notion that most people like kids' hand-published writing more than they like pieces published on a computer.

TIP:

THINGS TO THINK ABOUT WHEN YOU PUBLISH BY HAND

Let's assume that by some miracle I have convinced you to publish your next piece by hand. To make the most of your most excellent choice, I hope you'll at least consider the following:

- **Double-space, don't single-space.** Skipping a line between lines of text gives you a little extra room to fix mistakes. It also makes our writing easier to read.

- **Use pen, not pencil.** I know, I know. Pen can't be erased when you make a mistake. But pencil smears, and too many erasures look awful. Better to slow down, be careful, and use pen. It's more formal than pencil and it will communicate to your readers that you take your writing seriously. Stick with blue or black ink; red is typically used for corrections; other colors, like green or purple, look weird.

- **Use printing, not cursive.** Cursive writing is hard to read. That's all there is to it. These days, there are few times when we encounter cursive writing as readers. As a result, we're less familiar with it. Even in school where you probably learned cursive, you'll find your teachers requiring it less and less. Cursive handwriting is the perfect choice for personal correspondence and your signature. When writing other things by hand, stick with printing.

- **Use one side of the paper only.** When you get down to the last line at the bottom of a page, it's natural to want to flip it over and start again on the other side. Don't do it. Your piece will look nicer and be easier to read if you write on one side of the paper only.

- **Number your pages.** Double-spacing and writing on one side of the paper means your piece will likely balloon up to a larger number of pages than you were expecting. Make sure you number each one so both you and your readers can keep track of them. Page numbers are not required for a cover page, title page, or any "special" pages. Without getting into the rules of book production, you can assume the cover is page one and count forward from there. If you're curious about how this works in the real world, look at several books and see how publishers do it.

- **Make a cover.** Covers are cool. Get out some colored pencils, crayons, or felt pens (as long as they won't bleed through) and make the coolest cover you can. Look at several books to get ideas. Your title should be big and easy to read. Add an illustration that goes with your subject matter. And don't forget to put your name where everyone can see it.

- **Consider other "book" parts.** Grab a book off a shelf, especially a hardcover book, and look at all the things that are not part of the story itself. In addition to a front cover, there's a back cover with testimonials and a blurb that describes what the book is about. You'll also find things like dedication pages, "About the Author" pages, and sometimes even special notes about how the book was made. Adding some of these things to your work will show your readers you take it seriously and that you expect them to take it seriously, too.

Beyond the writing itself, there are many things that go into the publication of a piece of writing. Most of us never think about them, but they make a big difference in the way readers think about what they read. Do you have to do these things? Of course not. But I believe each of them adds to the success of your published piece.

HMM, I WONDER...

I just had an interesting thought. Every year or so, my publisher will probably release a new edition of this book. Each new edition will have small changes in it. We'll add things readers have requested, fix a few mistakes, and remove things that no longer seem appropriate. How many years will it be, I wonder, before I have to remove this section on publishing by hand because no one will be doing it anymore?

> ## *Miss Margot says*
>
> When I was in fourth grade, some friends of mine and I published a magazine of poetry. We had drawings and page numbers and we thought it was really cool, even though back then all we had to work with was a typewriter and this thing called a mimeograph machine. (Ask your parents!) I still have copies of these publications—even though the poetry is kind of embarrassing now. The fact that I saved this writing for more than thirty years should tell you something about how important publishing can be.

PUBLISHING BY COMPUTER

Almost everyone who writes today writes on a computer. That's just the way it is. So many things are much easier, especially when it comes to revising, editing, and publishing. And, frankly, it's a lot more fun.

I think the last time I wrote something without a computer was 1983. I was in college and one of the most popular gifts new college students received was their very own portable electric typewriter. With its erasable "self-correcting" ribbon and 250-character memory, it seemed like one cool machine at first. But it weighed about thirty pounds, was incredibly noisy, and sometimes ate the paper I was feeding it. For the $200 I think it cost, I probably used it five times before junking it in favor of the computers on the third floor of the university library.

One of the reasons my friends and I never thought of ourselves as publishers when we were growing up was because there was no way for us to create something that looked like it had been published. With improvements in computer hardware and software, this is no longer the case. Now anyone can produce writing that looks like the writing we see in books.

You aren't limited to publishing on paper either. Some writers write thousands of words a day that never end up on paper. These writers publish electronically, often on their own websites. They also write for online magazines and other digital publications. These days, I imagine you could have an entire career as a writer without ever publishing on paper.

THINGS TO THINK ABOUT WHEN YOU PUBLISH BY COMPUTER

There's a great feeling of power when you use a computer to publish your writing, but with that power comes responsibility. Most of that responsibility involves learning new things about how software works and how publishers make their writing look good.

TIP:

Here's some information that will put you on the path to better computer-based publishing:

- **Use the right fonts.** You probably have 500 fonts on your computer. About 493 of them should never be used for writing. The traditional font for text documents is Times. It's called a serif font because the lines that make up each character come to little points at the ends. Virtually all fonts used in books and magazines are serif fonts. If you don't like Times—and many people don't because it is so old and so overused—try other serif fonts that look similar. Fonts like Helvetica or Arial that do not have points on them are called sans serif fonts. While they aren't good for most of the text in your pieces, they do work well in larger sizes, and often with bold formatting, for headings and titles.

- **Watch your line spacing and line width.** Most word processors automatically give you a six-inch-long line to work with. This is too wide. If you look at most books, you'll notice that the width of a line rarely exceeds four-and-a-half inches. As for the amount of space between lines, our teachers in school often ask for double-spacing. But in books you'll notice that single spacing is what publishers use. The double-spaced tradition in school arose because teachers wanted space between the lines to make comments and corrections. Generally, when we publish our writing, we don't want people to make comments and corrections. As long as you're using the shorter line width I suggested, you don't need to double-space.

- **If you justify, hyphenate.** Most books have justified lines. This means that both the left and right sides of the text are even and smooth. If you decide to justify your margins, make sure you also turn on hyphenation. This makes justified text easier to read by telling the program you are using to put hyphens in words that are too big to fit at the ends of certain lines. Justification without hyphenation often leaves strange gaps between words that can make your writing hard to read.

- **Put only one space after a period.** If you were taught to type by some old person like me, you might have been taught to put two spaces after a period. That's what we learned in typing class back in the good old days. Computers, however, are not typewriters, so we don't need to leave the extra space anymore. Just put one space after a period and move on to the next sentence.

- **Avoid clip art.** I know it's tempting to insert a graphic here and there from all that wonderful clip art you have on your computer, but try to resist the temptation if you can. Clip art is cheesy. It really is. And what's more, everyone has exactly the same graphics. Do you really want to illustrate your unique way of writing with the same clip art everybody else uses? If you want art, create it yourself. Even if you aren't very good at drawing, I guarantee what you come up with will be better than clip art.

- **Make backups.** Publishing by hand has one distinct advantage over publishing by computer: you can't lose all your work when the system crashes or someone accidentally deletes your documents. There are many ways to make backups of your files, but one of my favorites is to e-mail whatever I'm working on to myself at the end of the day. Then I know I've got a backup copy saved in my e-mail account on someone else's computer. This is great because if my computer blows up, or somebody steals it, I won't lose my work.

This is not a comprehensive list of everything you need to know to publish great looking text, but it's a start. If you're really interested in layout, design, and typography, your best resource is a shelf full of books. Open up three or four and spend a few minutes comparing the design work of different publishers. Everything you need to know is there on the page.

Miss Margot says

My dad ran a printing company when I was in school, and I met a lot of cool people who designed great looking stuff. Besides looking at books, talk to your art teacher or friends of yours or your parents or people who design publications for a living. You might even get to meet someone in the art department of your local paper. These people can give you a ton of great tips for making your pieces look like professional publications.

TEN GREAT WAYS TO START PUBLISHING NOW

So what can you do if you want to move beyond publishing by hand or printing out your stories on a computer? A lot, as it turns out. There are more opportunities to publish writing now than there have ever been. And new opportunities are popping up all the time.

Thanks to technology, and to a dramatic increase in our society's interest in kids' writing, every writer, regardless of age, can publish. It may take time and a little ingenuity, but if you persevere, it'll happen.

Here's a list of ten ways to publish your writing:

1 **Build a website.** While not exactly a walk in the park, building your own website isn't rocket science either. The best part is that you don't even have to own software to do it because there are now many online services that let you use website-building tools for free. If you want a lot of control over how your writing is presented online, this is a good option to consider, even if it does take some extra work.

2 Start blogging. If you like the idea of having your own website but don't like the idea of having to set it up, try a blog instead. Blogs are a special kind of website that require almost no setup or maintenance. One of the neat things about blogs is that your readers can make comments back to you about your pieces. If you don't like this feature, don't worry. You can turn it off.

3 Publish to an e-mail list. It's easy to get e-mail addresses of people you know. It's also easy to put those addresses into one big group and send everyone the same message at once. That message could contain some writing of yours. People publish information to e-mail address lists all the time. While this doesn't have the same feeling of publishing your work on the Internet, it does allow you to control who gets to read your writing.

4 Create a newsletter. As an alternative to electronic publication, many people put out printed newsletters on a weekly, monthly, or quarterly basis. These publications typically focus on a particular theme or subject. Sometimes people organize them around a hobby or other interest. Then they send their newsletter to people who are interested in the same thing.

5 Put out a newspaper or magazine. This is my personal favorite. I love newspapers and magazines, and I think they're a lot of fun to put together. They take more work than a newsletter because they require more layout and design. But to me, that's part of what makes them fun. The best part, however, is how incredibly impressed people are when they read your first issue.

6 Submit stories to kids' publications. Many publications accept kids' writing. Some even pay. But even those that don't can help you get published. Just keep one thing in mind: if you do decide to submit something, remember that the publisher is under no obligation to accept it. Most pieces writers submit are not used. So don't get discouraged; sometimes perseverance is the best quality a writer can have.

Miss Margot says

Remember that anything you submit to a publication might look different once it appears in print. That's because editors are allowed to make small changes to your work. So be prepared.

7 **Enter contests.** Just as there are now many publications for kids' writing, there are many writing contests for kids, too. In most cases, the winning entries get published somewhere. Just be careful of one thing: some contest promoters will try to take your work by saying that they own it if you submit it for the contest. This really isn't fair, unless they're going to pay you for it, so read the entry requirements carefully.

8 **Send letters to the editor.** I do this all the time. If I read something in our local newspaper and I have a strong opinion about it—particularly if it's about education—I send in a letter to the editor. These letters are very short, typically 250 words or less, so they don't take much time. And every so often, one of my letters gets printed in the paper a few days later.

9 **Write editorials.** When I really have something to say, and 250 words just isn't enough for me to say it, I write an editorial and send it to the paper. At 750 words, I have plenty of room to stretch out and make my case. While many editorials are written by professional writers, most papers reserve at least one editorial spot per week for members of the community.

Miss Margot says

Newspapers and magazines love publishing well-written letters and op-eds from local school kids, so if you've got something to say about things in your school, your community, or even the entire country, this is a great way to make it public.

10 **Join your school paper.** Most middle and high schools have a school newspaper. Why not write for it? You'll get some terrific experience and have lots of people to help you with things like editing. The cool part, though, is seeing your stories in print and having everyone in your school see them, too.

Thanks to technology, and to a dramatic increase in our society's interest in kids' writing, there's no reason why any writer, regardless of age, should feel that he or she cannot be published in some way. It may take time and a little ingenuity, but if you persevere, it'll happen.

CHAPTER SEVEN

Be a Memoir Writer

TEN THINGS YOU NEED TO KNOW
EVEN IF YOU DON'T READ THIS CHAPTER

1   Writing a memoir is like taking a snapshot of a moment in your life that really mattered to you.

2   Even though we associate memoirs with politicians, movie stars, and other famous people, regular people like you and me write them all the time.

3   People love to read memoirs because it's human nature to want to know about other people's lives.

4   Most memoirs are about things that happen to us, but they can also be about places we've been or people we've known.

5   Both good and bad experiences can provide inspiration for memoirs.

6   In the best memoirs, writers give us a sense of how they were changed by their experiences.

7   In deciding where to begin or end a memoir, try to: tell as little of the story as possible in the most detailed way.

8   Once you've picked your topic and decided where to begin and end, identify your story's Big Moment. This will be the most important part.

9   When you get to the Big Moment, slow down the pacing by opening it up to reveal other moments inside and using more words to cover less time.

10   Writing a memoir is the process of turning memories into meaning, of taking something you see in your mind and turning it into something readers feel in their hearts.

EVERYBODY'S GOT A STORY TO TELL

Presidents do it after they leave office. Movie stars do it in the twilight of their careers. Prominent business executives do it after they've turned around big companies and made a bazillion dollars. But regular folks like you and me can do it, too. That's the great thing about writing memoirs.

Everybody's got a story to tell, and it's human nature to want to tell it. It's natural, too, for people to want to read our stories. This is what makes memoirs so popular: we all want to know what has happened to people we know.

But what exactly *is* a memoir? If the word "memoir" reminds you of the word "memory", you've already got the basic idea. What we're looking for here is a single important memory, a snapshot of a moment in your life that really mattered.

A MIDDLE-OF-THE-NIGHT MOMENT

When famous people tell their stories, they usually do it in huge books that span many years and require hundreds of pages. But that's not what we're after. We don't want a big book that tells our whole life story; we want a small piece that tells a story about a big moment in our life.

EXAMPLE:

Here's a story about a big moment in a young writer's life.

Middle of the Night Surprise

I woke up suddenly. Everything was blurry and I felt confused. It was pitch black, but I could hear footsteps on the creaky floor outside my bedroom. I held my breath as the footsteps walked past my door, around the corner, and into the living room.

➡️

Even though I was scared, I just had to get up out of bed to see what was happening. I don't know what I was thinking. If it was a burglar, I was in big trouble.

I took my time. I didn't want whatever it was to know that I was on its trail. I walked as lightly as I possibly could, but no matter how hard I tried, I still made noise. I slipped past my parents' room and entered the living room expecting to discover the intruder. I looked quickly from corner to corner but found nothing. Then I went into the kitchen.

At first, I didn't notice anything different. I wanted to turn on the light but I was too afraid. Then I saw it. At one end of the kitchen table there were three small boxes each wrapped with a different color paper.

Full of excitement, I quickly ran back to my brothers' room. I woke them up and brought them to the kitchen. We opened the boxes and found a single sheet of paper in each one. The first piece had little lines with symbols under them. The other two pieces were some kind of a key. After a few minutes, we figured it out: "On December 28th we are going to". The last part I spelled out loud. "D" "I" "S" "N" "E" "Y" "L" "A" "N" "D"!

My brothers and I exploded with excitement. We jumped for joy. We were thrilled out of our minds. We were also really noisy so that's when our parents got up. As they entered the kitchen, we all ran over and gave them a huge hug. What a great way to start a vacation.

I love the way the writer focuses on such a brief period of time. The whole story takes place over just a few minutes. It would have been easy to start earlier in the night, to talk about the Christmas season, or to go on after the big hug and tell us what happened next. But the writer chose instead to capture just this brief moment. And I think she chose wisely.

A MOMENT OF PAIN AND FEAR

In this next example, a writer recounts a memory he probably wishes he could forget. Everyone's life is a mixture of good things and bad things. Both provide inspiration for great memoirs.

EXAMPLE:

A Jog and a Dog

I was out on my regular evening jog. It was the beginning of fall and leaves swirled down around me and crunched under my feet as I headed toward a gigantic tree trunk where I often took a rest. I sat there for a few minutes, just looking around, and then I noticed it was getting dark so I decided to head for home.

As I stood up, I saw something crouching across the road. I took a step back, it took a step forward. At that moment my curiosity was greater than my fear so I stepped forward again to get a closer look. And then I laughed at myself. It was Chocolate, a friendly Lab that belonged to our neighbor. I'd known him for years. Sighing with relief, I reached down to pet him but stopped short as a low rumble in his throat grew to a loud growl.

I pulled my hand back and stepped away. That wasn't like Chocolate, I thought. I watched him for a moment and he watched me. Then I shrugged my shoulders, turned, and walked away. A few seconds later, I heard the clicking of paws on the pavement. Thinking nothing of it, I started running, but Chocolate was now running with me. I was scared.

When Chocolate started to growl again, I broke into a sprint. And that's when he bit me, right through my sweat suit and deep into the flesh of my thigh.

I fell to the ground screaming in horrible pain. There was blood everywhere. A man came over wondering what all the noise was about. Kicking at the dog, the man tried to get him away from me without getting bitten himself. After a few seconds that seemed like hours, Chocolate gave up and ran off.

Someone must have called 911 because the police showed up a few minutes later. I told them what had happened and they took me to the emergency room.

As I rode to the hospital, I tried to figure out why a friendly dog I'd known for years would suddenly attack me. The next day I found out that Chocolate had rabies. Our neighbor had to put him to sleep. Over the next few weeks, I got a series of painful shots and several stitches. And that was the end of it.

Except it wasn't the end. It's two years later. My injuries healed a long time ago. You can hardly even see the scar. But I don't jog at night anymore and I don't get close to dogs, not even friendly ones I've known for years.

In the best memoirs, the writer gives us a sense of how he or she was changed by an experience. I think this writer does a great job of that here. Being attacked by a dog at night is an extremely unsettling thing. And this writer shows us that he suffered not only physical pain in the moment but also emotional pain that may last the rest of his life.

FAMILY MOMENTS

Though memoirs are most often about things that happen to us, they can also be written about people we've known or places we've been.

EXAMPLE:

Here's a piece from a young writer about a summer cabin where her family enjoyed many wonderful vacations.

Our Family Cabin at the Beach

Sometimes, if I close my eyes, I can make believe it's summer and I'm back at our family cabin at the beach. I can see the waves rolling over the squishy sand, feel the sand squishing in between my toes, and laugh at the way my little brother picks up barnacle-covered rocks so he can watch the sand crabs scurry away.

Everyone in the family enjoys our time together at the beach. My aunt and uncle, cousins, grandma and grandpa, everybody comes to stay with us and enjoy the summer. Every morning we check to see what the tide brought in. Then we go exploring to look for special rocks. During the days we swim and sun tan.

In the afternoons, we play volleyball or badminton. Sometimes we just lay out in the sun and read. At night, we snuggle up in our blankets and toast marshmallows over the campfire while dad and grandpa tell scary stories.

The most fun for me is when dad gets out the big boat and the outboard motor and several of us go fishing. We have to get up really early, but I don't mind. Mostly we catch cod and flounder, but once my dad caught a twenty-pound salmon. I hooked one that was even bigger, but it broke my line and got away.

It seems like there's always something fun to do at the cabin. I don't think I've ever been bored. But I think it's just being with my family that makes it special. It's the only time each year that we're all together.

> It's always sad when it's time to go because none of us wants to leave. We say our goodbyes. We talk about all the fun we had. Then everyone drives away. As our car pulls out of the driveway, I turn to look out the back window. I think I'm afraid that if we go away, the cabin will go away, too. I try to look at everything so I can remember everything about it. Then I close my eyes so I can keep the memory with me until we come back again next year.

This kind of memoir is a little harder to write than the other two. Writing about people and places is often more challenging than writing about something that happened because there's no sequence of events to order the story.

The authors of "Middle of the Night Surprise" and "A Jog and a Dog" have only to tell their stories from beginning to end. The author of "Our Family Cabin at the Beach" has to work harder to find a way of organizing her piece. Because she couldn't use time, she decided to use activities. Each part of the story describes a different thing her family does while they visit the cabin, right up to the final activity when everybody heads for home.

Writing about people and places seems harder to me than writing about events for another a reason: events are easier for readers to relate to. For example, even if we've never been bitten by a dog while jogging, it's easy for us to understand the fear and other feelings someone might have in that situation. And who hasn't been surprised by an unexpected gift at some time in their life?

But how can we help our audience understand a person they've never known or a place they've never visited? The answer, of course, is to use details—and lots of them. If you decide to write a memoir about a place or a person, be aware that you may need extra detail to help your readers feel the same way you do about it. When you write about an event, on the other hand, the story itself may be enough to entertain the audience.

Miss Margot says

Think your life's too boring for a memoir? Can't remember anything exciting or interesting that's ever happened to you? Write about that. Even a boring life can make a good story if it's written in an entertaining way.

THE MAKING OF A MEMORY

One of the fascinating things about memories is that we make them up after the fact. Something happens to us and while it's happening we're aware of it, but we don't end up with a detailed memory of what happened until later, often when someone asks us to tell them what we experienced. As we tell the story, we talk about some parts and leave out others. In this simple process, the telling shapes the way we think about things. If we tell a story often enough, we're more likely to remember how we've told it than what actually occurred.

In a sense, we're all natural born storytellers because every time we think of something that has happened to us, we "tell" the story to our-selves in the process of trying to recall what happened. No matter what happens to us, or how good our memories are, there's no way we can ever remember something exactly as it happened. Many details get lost simply because they seem unimportant to us, while others get remem-bered differently because our memory isn't perfect.

The fact that our memories might change over time doesn't mean we're not good at remembering things, or that we intentionally try to make up lies. It just means we have a normal human brain that latches onto some parts of a story and lets other parts go. The changing nature of memory is one of the reasons why writing memoirs is so important: writing down a memory may be the only way to keep it. It may also be the best way to share it with others.

FRAMING A MEMORY

As you think about events in your life that might make great memoirs, think back to Chapter One where we did an exercise that involved writing down some of the unusual things that have happened in your life. This is a great way to come up with topics based on important events.

After you've decided on a suitable topic, you've got another important decision to make: How much of this story are you going to tell? Every event in your life is linked to the event that came before it and the event that comes after it. So how do you know where to start and where to end?

I call this "framing," and often I'm not sure how to do it in my own writing until I've been working on a piece for quite some time. My general rule is this: tell as little of the story as possible in the most detailed way. Memoirs usually work best when they are concentrated tightly around a single point of interest. In "Middle of the Night Surprise," that point was the deciphering of the message about the trip to Disneyland. In "A Jog and a Dog," it was the attack. Both writers did a good job of framing their stories, starting just a few minutes before the most interesting moment and ending shortly thereafter.

In "Our Family Cabin at the Beach," the writer didn't have a single event to focus us on because her story was about a place and a group of people. So instead of using points in the narrative to frame her story, she used a technique some people call bookending, where the beginning and end of the story are closely related and thereby frame everything in between:

> Sometimes, if I close my eyes, I can make believe it's summer and I'm back at our family cabin at the beach.
>
> …
>
> Then I close my eyes so I can keep the memory with me until we come back again next year.

Here, the writer uses the closing of her eyes and the recollection of a memory as her bookend device. I think it works nicely because it's simple, believable, and makes for a satisfying finish.

MORE THAN JUST MOMENTS

Though it's probably most natural to write memoirs about a single event, person, or place, we can often make our stories richer if we bring in relevant details about other elements. For example, in "Our Family Cabin at the Beach," the story might have been even better if the writer had given us some details about her family members.

One of my favorite parts is right here at the beginning:

> I can see the waves rolling over the squishy sand, feel the sand squishing in between my toes, and laugh at the way my little brother picks up barnacle-covered rocks so he can watch the sand crabs scurry away.

What I'm most drawn to here is the part about her little brother. I don't know how old he is, but I get the impression that maybe he's five and that he's at that really curious age where he'll go poking into just about anything to find out what it is. It might be fun to learn more about him.

Later on, there's a hint of a good story:

> The most fun for me is when dad gets out the big boat and the outboard motor and several of us go fishing. We have to get up really early, but I don't mind. Mostly we catch cod and flounder, but once my dad caught a twenty-pound salmon. I hooked one that was even bigger, but it broke my line and got away.

Catching and losing a big fish could make for a great story within the story. Of course, the entire piece would be much longer with these additions (and now you can see why people spend hundreds of pages on their memoirs) but the story might also be richer and more successful, too.

THE PERFECT PAPER MEMORY

With memoir, more than almost any other kind of writing, I find it hard to make judgments about what to include and exclude. I have this sense that I want to get the story "just right" as though there's some perfect way of putting it on paper. There isn't, of course. And I've often proven that to myself, and to the students I've worked with, by writing the same piece two completely different ways. But I still get stuck on the idea that a particular story has to be told a particular way.

The best way out of this for me has been to stop thinking about how I want to tell the story and think instead about how others want to hear it. For example, I write often for the students I work with in school, and it just makes sense to vary the details of a story according to the age of my audience.

So perhaps our audience provides the answer to the problem of creating the perfect paper memory. If we can't get the story right for ourselves, we can try to get it right for them.

Miss Margot says

I come from a long line of Southern storytellers, and one thing I learned from listening to stories over and over is that if you can whittle down your story to just the very best details—the stuff that will make people ooh and ahh—you're more likely to get it right. But getting there isn't always easy (though it's often fun). You have to tell your story many times to find out where the best parts are. Then the next time you tell the story, you leave out the parts nobody seemed to care about and improve the parts they did. After a while, you've got an awesome piece. It's the same when you write a memoir. Write a lot, then pare it down based on the feedback you get from readers.

THE MOMENT OF A MEMORY

Memoirs based on a single event often turn on a single moment— when a rabid dog bites you in the leg, or when you discover you'll soon be heading off to Disneyland. I like to think of this as the story's Big Moment. To tell the story well, we not only have to remember that moment accurately, we also have to handle it effectively in relation to all the other moments.

CAN YOU GIVE US A HINT?

Sometimes, right at the top of a story, the writer will give us a sense of what's to come. A common beginning I've seen many times goes something like this: "Last week something happened that changed my life forever." Obviously, at some point later on, the writer will tell us what that something was.

Now, I wouldn't say this beginning is bad. But every time I see it, I wonder if it's really necessary. As I read the first paragraph or two, I'll probably be able to figure out that I'm reading a memoir. And when the Big Moment comes, won't I also understand how the writer's life was changed as a result?

There is one situation where I think giving a hint about the Big Moment might be useful, and that's if the piece is very long. If your story runs to several thousand words, you'll be asking your reader to stay with you for quite a while as it develops. But what if the reader wants to go play a video game or run to the store for a candy bar or work on his stamp collection? Faced with competition like this, a good hint might be the thing that keeps your reader from booting up his PlayStation or running off to stick stamps in an album.

A PACE FOR EVERYTHING AND EVERYTHING IN ITS PACE

Pacing is a hard concept to talk about and an even harder one to understand. But I'll give it a try if you will.

In "A Jog and a Dog," the story starts with the writer jogging and ends with the writer being taken to the hospital. How much time passes during this story? We can't say for sure, but twenty to thirty minutes seems like a reasonable guess.

Take a look at how the writer spends some of that time at the beginning:

> I was out on my regular evening jog. It was the beginning of fall and leaves swirled down around me and crunched under my feet as I headed toward a gigantic tree trunk where I often took a rest. I sat there for a few minutes, just looking around, and then I noticed it was getting dark so I decided to head for home.

With some jogging, some resting, and a minute or so to decide to go home, we can imagine that perhaps as much as half the total time of the story may have passed in this first paragraph.

Now take a look at how time passes during the Big Moment:

> When Chocolate started to growl again, I broke into a sprint. And that's when he bit me, right through my sweat suit and deep into the flesh of my thigh.
>
> I fell to the ground screaming in horrible pain. There was blood everywhere. A man came over wondering what all the noise was about. Kicking at the dog, the man tried to get him away from me without getting bitten himself. After a few seconds that seemed like hours, Chocolate gave up and ran off.

How long is this? Thirty seconds? A minute? Compared to the opening paragraph, the writer covers much less time, but includes much more action. He also uses about twenty more words. This is how pacing works: writers speed things up by covering more time with less words or they slow things down by covering less time with more words.

How do writers decide when to slow things down or speed things up? In general, the more important something is, the slower the writer wants to go. Why? Because when writers have something important to say, they want to make sure you read it.

Miss Margot says,

Sometimes, writers speed up important things, like action. If you want your reader to know that something happened really quickly, or that a million things were happening at once, you might use shorter sentences so it reads like it feels. If you want your reader to feel time drag—the old "minutes felt like hours" thing—then use more words so the reader has to slow down with you. The best way to see if you've got the pacing you want is to read your piece out loud.

OPENING UP A MOMENT

For most writers, moving quickly through a scene is easy. It's slowing down that's hard. But if the Big Moment really is just a moment, how can you make it any slower than it actually is? Once again, the answer is in the details. (All the answers seem to be in the details, don't they?) In this particular case, however, we have to solve an additional problem: Where are the details supposed to come from?

I started running and a dog bit me. There, I'm done. I decoded a message and found out I was going to Disneyland. There, I'm done. What can we do with this? How can we make the Big Moment bigger? By opening it up and letting readers see what's inside.

Let me show you what I'm talking about by opening up a story I've been working on. Remember back in Chapter Two when I was talking about fishing with my dad? There's a story I want to tell about a strange day when I caught something like ten fish in about twenty minutes.

The Big Moment I want to capture was the very first fish I caught that day. Normally, I'd cast out my line, put my pole down, and wait half an hour for nothing to happen. But this time, the fish struck a few seconds after my bait hit the water.

I could certainly write it this way:

> I cast my bait out into the lake and five seconds later hooked a fish.

Or I can open up that moment like this:

> I flipped the bail on my reel and turned to look back over my right shoulder. Like I'd done a thousand times before, I whipped my rod back and forth letting the line go at just the right moment. For a couple of seconds, I followed the arc of my sinker as it flew through the air and plunked into the water about seventy-five feet in front of me. Without even thinking about it, I moved the reel handle forward, clicked back the bail, and leaned over to put my rod down and wait. But before I could get the rod into the holder, I felt the line go taut. What in the world's goin' on? I thought to myself. My bait couldn't have even hit bottom yet. Then the rod jumped out of my hand as a rainbow trout broke water in front of me.

Besides adding extra words, can you see what I'm doing here? I'm taking the casting from the first example and opening that moment up by describing the moments inside. Then I'm taking the moment of hooking the fish and opening that up, too.

TIP:

Within any moment, big or small, there are more moments. We change the pace of our writing by deciding how much we want to open them up. In general, we speed up for things that don't matter much and slow down for the important stuff.

BE A WRITER LIKE KAILE SHILLING

Kaile Shilling is a grant writer by profession. She works for a nonprofit organization that helps former gang members in Los Angeles, CA. In her free time, she writes screenplays.

WHAT KIND OF WRITER ARE YOU?

I'm not as disciplined a writer as I'd like to be. Maybe that makes me a lazy writer. Most of my writing is spec screenplays, which is challenging, as there is no deadline, and only the hope that someone will be interested in it at the end. So perhaps I'm an eternally optimistic writer. Professionally, I write grants for a nonprofit, which keeps the writing muscles in shape, as grant writing is really a form of storytelling about the organization and the work being done.

WHY DO YOU WRITE?

I love words. I love the power of words, the impact they can have, the beauty of finding precisely the right combination of words. I also love writing because there is a necessary gap between the writer and the reader—the reader fills in the spaces with his or her imagination, so the experience of having read something is a collaborative one, a joint journey that is uniquely personal for each reader. Film is also a necessarily collaborative art form, which is probably why I love it and love writing for it.

Q WHAT MADE YOU WANT TO BE A WRITER?

A Reading great books and great essays and great plays made me want to write. Spending afternoons in my room unable to put down a book, acting in plays where I reveled in the spoken word, and spending time dissecting all of the above to unravel and explore the different levels of meaning, the metaphors, the symbols, the imagery—all those things that can get packed into even the simplest writing. Plus, there's something eternal about the captured word, and I think deep down that all of us want to touch a part of that sense of eternity.

Q WHAT ADVICE WOULD YOU GIVE TO A FELLOW WRITER WHO WAS JUST STARTING OUT?

A Write, write, write, write, write. Write bad stuff, write terrible stuff, write sloppy stuff, just write it. The hardest part of writing is the writing. Once it's out, editing and improving are much easier. Get something on the page, and get yourself used to writing.

THE FEELING OF A MEMORY

What makes something worth remembering? Why do we remember some things as clearly as the moment they happened and others not at all? If you want to be a memoir writer, these are questions worth thinking about. And for once, I'm happy to say, the answer is not in the details.

The reason some memories last forever and others don't seems to be the way we feel about them. In general, the stronger the feeling, the longer the memory lasts. The same thing is true when we share our memories with others. When the people we share our stories with feel strongly about them, our memories last longer in their memory, too.

ONCE MORE WITH FEELING

Feelings are the key to writing great memoirs. Even though the story is about what happened, it's not really what happened that matters. It's how you feel about it and how you convey those feelings to your readers.

But how do we work with our feelings in a memoir? Aren't they just there because of what happened? Yes, they are. Our feelings are inside of us as part of the memory we're trying to recall. But we have to work a bit to get them down on the page.

HOW WE FEEL ABOUT A MEMOIR

Of the three memoirs we've looked at in this chapter, I think the one about the dog attack is the most successful. Surprisingly, it's not the one I identify with most easily. Nothing like that has ever happened to me. In contrast, I spent many summers at a family cabin that sounds almost exactly like the one described in that piece. And I've received special presents under unusual circumstances like the kids in the other story. You'd think I'd like those pieces more. But I don't.

The reason I like "A Jog and a Dog" better than the other two is because of how I feel about the ending:

> It's two years later. My injuries healed a long time ago. You can hardly even see the scar. But I don't jog at night anymore and I don't get close to dogs, not even friendly ones I've known for years.

What moves me here is that the writer has gone beyond the surface feelings of the attack—surprise, pain, and confusion—to the deep feelings of fear, resentment, and regret that make this event memorable even two years after it happened. That's hard to do. And there's no technique I can offer to help you do it. Writing like this comes from knowing yourself and from being able to be honest about who you are, what you think, and how you feel.

THE MEANING OF A MEMORY

Feelings are important in all writing and memoir is no exception. But there's something else that matters, too: meaning. Meaning is a tricky thing because it's not something we're used to thinking about. Stuff happens to us all the time, but we rarely sit around afterward saying things like, "Wow, that was interesting. I wonder what it means?"

But readers will.

Readers are meaning-making machines. They're always asking, "What did the author mean by that?" and "What does that mean to me?" If they don't find what they're looking for, they have a tendency to look for it somewhere else—somewhere that isn't the piece you wrote.

You'd think that if something were so important it would be easy to describe. Not so with meaning. I'm sure one of your Language Arts teachers could tell you about it. Or I could give you the definition out of the dictionary. But I don't think you'd be any closer to figuring it out. So instead I'll make up my own way of explaining it.

To me, understanding the meaning of a piece of writing means answering three questions:

- **What's the one most important thing the writer wants the reader to know?** There's almost always one thing the writer wants the reader to know that's more important than anything else in the piece. This is a significant part of the meaning. Without asking the author, we can never know for certain what this is, but we can make an educated guess. In "Our Family Cabin at the Beach," for example, I would wager that the author's one most important thing has something to do with how much she loves her family and how glad she is to have a place where they can all be together.

- **Why did the writer write this?** Although it may seem this way at times, writers don't just write about any old thing for no reason at all. A piece of writing represents a significant investment of time and energy. And when it's a memoir, it also represents an investment of heart. Think about the memoir I'm trying to write about fishing with my dad. Some of my memories of my father aren't good ones, but I'm still trying to write about them. Why? Because they're meaningful to me. Part of the meaning of what we create comes from why we work so hard to create it.

- **Why should the reader care?** This is the toughest question of all and probably the most important to answer. It's not enough just for us to care about our writing. Our readers have to care about it, too. That means we have to give them something to care about. The nature of a memoir makes this hard. After all, it's your life, why should someone else care about it? No matter how many times I've thought about that question, I've always come up with the same answer: the best reason a reader would have to care about someone else's life is because, in one way or another, it resembles their own. That means we have to give our readers something they can identify with, something that makes them say, "Hey, that reminds me of…"

Meaning is a tricky thing. It isn't easily tied down or bottled up. Sometimes it can't be determined at all with a reasonable degree of certainty. Memories are tricky, too. They come and go, sometimes vivid, sometimes blurry. Writing a memoir is the process of turning memories into meaning, of taking something you see in your mind and turning it into something readers feel in their hearts.

CHAPTER EIGHT

Be an Essay Writer

TEN THINGS YOU NEED TO KNOW
EVEN IF YOU DON'T READ THIS CHAPTER

1 An essay is a brief, informal piece in which a writer presents a unique and personal view on a narrowly focused topic of his or her choice.

2 Essays are all about individual expression, your way of looking at the world and how that way differs from everyone else's.

3 The essay became a popular form of writing because the invention of the printing press made it possible for individual writers to begin publishing their work and distributing it to large audiences.

4 One tradition among essay writers is to explore normal or otherwise unimportant parts of life in sensational and often humorous ways.

5 The best serious essays are those that challenge our beliefs and invite us to consider a different and often unconventional view.

6 Most essay writing would probably be called expository writing in school.

7 Because the term "expository writing" is often hard for people to define, ask your teachers to show you examples of what they mean when they ask you to do it.

8 The essence of expository writing is exposure: the idea is to expose your ideas. This means you have to show what you know by explaining what you think and why you think it.

9 The term "expository writing" is rarely used outside of school. In the real world, when people want you to create a kind of writing, they show you what kind they mean by giving you an example.

10 There are three keys to a successful essay: insightful ideas that make readers think, interesting details that encourage readers to trust your observations, and an inviting voice that feels like a real person talking.

AN HONORABLE TRADITION

"Today, Class, I would like each of you to write an expository essay on"
—Stop right there!

This is not what we're going to be talking about in this chapter.

While it's certainly true that anyone who has been in school past the third grade has probably been asked to write essays like this many times, the kind of essay I want to talk about is very different. And though it can be hard at times to define exactly what an essay is, we can be sure that it is most certainly *not* an assignment given by a teacher where every student is forced to write on the same topic in the same way at the same time.

The kind of essay we're talking about here is a brief, informal piece in which a writer presents a unique and personal view on a narrowly focused topic of his or her choice. Essays are all about individual expression, your way of looking at the world and how that way differs from everyone else's. It's all about you: your topic, your angle, your ideas. It's also about the audience you're trying to reach, the people you are writing to, and why you want them to consider what you have to say.

MORE GREAT MOMENTS IN WRITING HISTORY (OH, BOY!)

It seems people didn't start writing essays until the end of the sixteenth century. Now, obviously, people had their own unique and personal views of things long before then. So what inspired them to start producing this particular kind of writing all of a sudden? The invention of the printing press probably had a lot to do with it.

Think about it for a second: if you're a person who wants to share your ideas in written form with other people, you need to have a way of producing and distributing multiple copies of what you write. If you're not as rich as a king, you have to do this in a way that isn't too expensive. And if you plan to publish anything that might be critical of your society, you need a way of publishing you can access without permission from the powers that be. Prior to the invention of the printing press, these requirements were hard to meet.

Until the printing press was in widespread use, production and distribution of the printed word was controlled almost entirely by governments, religious groups, or wealthy people who were probably running governments and religious groups. Back then, publishing meant punching your pieces out of stone or leather, or commanding a legion of personal scribes to do your copying. Needless to say, these circumstances didn't inspire individuals of more humble means to pen their grand observations about life. Even if they wrote something good, making and distributing multiple copies of it was extremely difficult. But developments in printing technology changed all that, and eventually the essay became a popular way of putting new ideas out into the world.

EXPRESSIONS OF A UNIQUE PERSONALITY

Not every essayist strives to change the world with words. Most, in fact, strive only to capture small parts of their experience in interesting and entertaining ways. It's their unusual perspective that draws us to them as writers and their unique personality that draws us to them as people.

EXAMPLE:

Here's an essay I like a lot. I love the light-hearted but dramatic way the writer takes a common social situation and blows it way out of proportion.

The Last Stick of Gum

If you see a person chewing gum, isn't it normal to want some, too? And if that person is a friend of yours, isn't it normal to ask them for some? Maybe. But good luck getting it. Every time I ask, my friends just say, "Sorry, this is my last stick."

I have gone days without someone giving me a stick of gum and then, for no apparent reason, sticks seem to be everywhere. It's as if, on certain days known only to gum manufacturers, you can hear people saying on playgrounds and in lunchrooms all over America, "Who wants gum?" Perhaps these people have discovered a secret government warehouse full of single sticks. Maybe they feel guilty about not sharing in the past. Or maybe they just want to confuse us.

But soon we see the method in their madness. Our problem seems small at first: we can't seem to focus in class; we miss the winning shot at 3-on-3; we lose a homework assignment and even forget to lie about it. Then it hits us: we want gum. We need gum. We have to have gum.

We race around the playground looking for our gum-chewing friends, but they are nowhere to be found. Desperate, we approach a stranger chewing happily away: "Please, I beg you! I must have a piece of gum!" To which the stranger replies, "Sorry, this is my last stick."

There's a wonderful tradition among essayists of writing pieces that explore normal or otherwise unimportant parts of life in sensational and often humorous ways. I love pieces like these and am always encouraging the students I work with to write them. Too often, though, we think we have to be funny to write something like this. But that isn't true. Our everyday lives are funny enough. We just have to find some little thing we experience all the time and put it under the microscope of our imagination. When we take something normal and distort it, making it bigger and more dramatic than it really is, the humor pops up on its own.

THE SERIOUS SIDE OF LIFE

Of course, essayists have their serious sides, too. And this is where, it seems to me, they have the greatest potential to change the way their readers look at things. In my opinion, the best serious essays are those that challenge our normal beliefs and invite us to consider different, and often unconventional, points of view.

EXAMPLE:

In the essay below, a writer takes on the conventional notion of what it's like to grow up. Growing up is supposed to be something kids—especially kids in high school—look forward to. Everyone it seems is eager to win their independence and start living their real lives outside of school and away from home. Everyone except the author of this essay.

What Do I Have To Look Forward To?

I've never understood why so many of my friends were in such a hurry to grow up. When I look around at the adults I know, growing up doesn't seem like much fun. My parents always seem worried about things. If it's not me or my brother, it's the house or the car or work, or something having to do with one of their parents.

Other adults don't seem much happier either. My friends' parents seem to have just as many problems to deal with. Whenever I visit after school, the moms look tired, and you can forget about even talking to the dads for a couple of hours after they get home from work, if they even get home at all. (In fact, I don't think I've ever met the fathers of some of my friends. It's as though they don't even exist.)

I'm not saying that every adult I know is like this. It's just that most adults never seem to really be able to enjoy anything without worrying about it, too. No matter what I'm doing with my parents, they always seem bothered by the thought that something bad might happen, or that they might be doing something wrong. Sometimes things do go wrong, but mostly things turn out okay. Nothing really bad has ever happened in our family, but my parents always seem nervous about things, or unsure of themselves, as though they don't really know what they're doing.

From my point of view, being an adult doesn't look so good. Get up, go to work, come home, go to sleep, try to get the kids to do whatever it is you want them to do. And on the weekends maybe you get up a little later, but it's basically the same thing: work around the house, take care of the kids, etc. Who wants to do that? I look at everything my parents have to do and I wonder what's the point? Is this really what I have to look forward to?

I guess it's hard being an adult. When you're an adult, you're in the middle, and there's no one to help you out on either end. You've got kids *and* parents to take care of, and nobody around to take care of you.

I guess the hardest part for me in imagining what life will be like when I grow up is looking at all the adults I know now and not seeing anyone who seems really happy. I don't know a single adult who likes their job: my mom and dad don't, my friends' parents don't, and I don't think my teachers do either. All I ever hear from adults are complaints. And even though I know most parents really love their children, they don't seem to show it very much, and so I wonder if having children is really as terrific as everyone says it is.

Everybody's always talking about adults being good role models for kids, but maybe kids should be models for them. Maybe we could teach them a few things about how to have a good time and enjoy life. It's worth a try. I'd hate to think that the way growing up seems to me now is the way it's going to be when I get there.

Now there's a different way of looking at things. And that's exactly the point. If memoir writers want us to feel, essay writers want us to think. They want us to think that their unusual viewpoint is something we might at least consider and possibly even agree with. They know they have an uphill battle given that they've intentionally taken an unconventional position. But it's a battle worth fighting because they feel they are defending the truth.

STRIKING A BALANCE

While some essays try to describe the truth for everyone, others try to describe it just for the essay writer. Rather than looking outward at life and at the world, these essays turn inward as writers look at themselves.

EXAMPLE:

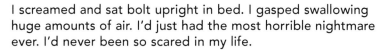

Here, a younger writer also writes about growing up. But she does it in a light-hearted way I think we can all identify with.

When I Grow Up

I tried to run, but I couldn't. The monster seemed like it was growing by the minute. And then, the most horrible thing was about to happen—

I screamed and sat bolt upright in bed. I gasped swallowing huge amounts of air. I'd just had the most horrible nightmare ever. I'd never been so scared in my life.

Still gasping, I called "Mom!"

My mom came sleepily into my bedroom and sat on the edge of my bed. "What is it, sweetie?" she asked, her voice full of concern.

Tears welled up in my eyes as I remembered the ghostly monster from my dream. "I...I had a nightmare," I finally managed to say.

"Poor thing," my mom said sympathetically as she gave me a hug. "But don't worry," she added. "You will stop having them when you grow up."

I nodded my head in agreement, although inside I secretly felt that I wouldn't. After my mom left, I laid on my pillows and started to think.

People mostly grownups were always telling me that
things would happen, or that I would like something better
when I was "grown up." Apparently, they thought being
grown up meant liking everything and knowing everything.
Well I most certainly did not! To me, growing up meant having
responsibility and trying to make good choices.

I wondered if my life would be different as a grownup. I knew
I would be older and more mature, but would I be prettier?
Fatter? Skinnier? Would I choose to get married? Or get a
job?

Then I realized something. I was twleve years old. Right now
none of that stuff mattered. I didn't need a husband because
I had older siblings. I didn't need a job because my mom and
dad provided for me. The only job I had right now was to be
a kid. And that was just what I was going to do.

My favorite part is right at the end when the writer cuts herself off
from worrying about adult life by remembering that she's only twelve.
She's taking on a serious topic, but she isn't so serious about it that
she can't look at herself and admit that she's acting like her own worst
enemy and causing the very problem she's concerned about. We all act
that way at times, don't we? And that's why I think this piece is successful: the writer shows us a side of herself we can relate to.

YOU HAVE TO SHOW WHAT YOU KNOW

I was hoping to avoid this topic, but it reared its ugly head at the start
of the chapter when I threw in that line from the teacher that said,
"Today, Class, I would like each of you to write an expository essay
on—"

I've mentioned before that sometimes we have odd ways of doing
things in school, ways that don't match up well with how things are
done in the real world. In school, sometimes we use words for things

that are different from the words we encounter in our real lives. "Expository" is one of those words. After you leave school, you'll probably never hear it again. But while you're there, it can be helpful to at least try and figure out what teachers mean when they say it.

EXPOSING MY IGNORANCE

When I was in school, expository writing darn near killed me. I never understood what the word "expository" really meant, and as I got older I just got more confused. Whenever a teacher told me to write it, I just faked my way along and hoped for the best.

Fortunately, once I got out of school, I never had to give it another thought. I've written professionally for almost twenty years (tech writing, journalism, business plans, brochures, scripts, books, you name it) and not once has anyone ever asked me for a piece of expository writing, which is a nice thing because I still wouldn't know what they were talking about.

The problem is that the term is too general. Some teachers I've talked to think expository writing is the same as research writing. Some think of it as any kind of factual writing. Still others think of it even more generally than that as any kind of writing where the writer explains something to the reader. (But doesn't all writing involve explaining? This is the definition that confused me most when I was a kid.)

LET ME SHOW YOU WHAT I MEAN

After years of trying to figure this out—as a student, as a teacher, and as a professional writer—I've simply decided to give up and make my own definition. The way I look at it, the essence of expository writing is exposure: the idea is to expose your ideas. But there's more to it than simply saying, "Here's my idea." In addition to exposing your thoughts, you must also expose your thinking. This means showing your readers how you reached your conclusions. To expose something is to show it. So I think of expository writing as showing what you know.

When it comes to defining expository writing in school, I'm not sure your experience will be much different than mine was. Every teacher you have will probably define expository writing a little differently. That's just the way it is; no one is trying to play a trick on you. So what do you do?

If a teacher asks you to do some expository writing, but you don't know exactly what he's talking about, ask him to show you what he knows about it by presenting you with models you can study. Rather than telling you to "write an expository essay on…", your teachers should show you exactly what they're looking for by giving you finished examples of the kind of writing they want and even writing something themselves right in front of you. Then it doesn't matter which names they use or how they define them because you've got something real right in front of you everyone can agree on.

This is how it's done in the real world. When someone wants someone else to produce a piece of writing, they say something like, "I need you to write one of those," and if there's even the slightest confusion, they show you what "one of those" is.

EXAMPLE:

When my publisher asked me to write this book, he and I talked about producing something similar to other books we both knew. To find examples, we looked online and went to bookstores. We also looked at a couple of the books he had published in the past. I even wrote a few pages of the first chapter to provide an example of what I could do. For several weeks, we made an effort to show each other the kind of book we were thinking of so that everyone involved in this project would know exactly what we were doing.

BE A WRITER LIKE DAN HULL

Dan Hull teaches high school in Phoenix, Arizona. He has been doing this for many years, maybe even longer than you have been alive. Unlike most teachers, Mr. Hull teaches his classes at night, which means when you are in class at 8:00AM, he is sleeping. As an English teacher, his focus is writing.

Q

WHAT KIND OF WRITER ARE YOU?

A

I am a storyteller and writing is one of the ways in which I tell stories. Even in expository writing like this interview, I see the process as a story. In this case, it is the story of me as a writer.

Q

WHY DO YOU WRITE?

A

I write because I have to. When I say I have to, it's not because someone is making me write. I have to write in the same way that other people have to create music or paint or play basketball. To me, words are the keys to thinking. Writing gets the words out that are banging around inside my head. It's a way of taking thoughts and making them sit still.

Q

WHAT MADE YOU WANT TO BE A WRITER?

A

I have always loved words—the sounds, the feel, the flow. I believe that all human beings have a need to be creative in some way. For me, writing has always been a way to take what is happening inside of me and make it into something interesting outside of me. Some people create pictures with paint. I paint pictures with words.

Q

WHAT ADVICE WOULD YOU GIVE TO A FELLOW WRITER WHO WAS JUST STARTING OUT?

A

Keep writing. Like most skills, your writing will get better if you keep at it. I recently decided that I wanted to learn how to sew by hand and asked a friend to teach me. As I was sewing, stitch by stitch, I realized that every move I was making was wrong. Compared to the speed and beauty with which my friend was moving as she sewed, everything I was doing felt like a mistake, but I kept sewing anyway. I know that the only way to really learn how to sew is to keep sewing, and that with each crooked stitch, I am learning to someday create straight stitches.

SHOW OF SUPPORT

Though I'm sure some teachers would disagree with me, if I were in school I would classify each of the essays we've read in this chapter as expository. Outside of school it doesn't matter what we call them. The only thing that matters is whether or not they're any good.

You can guess that I probably wouldn't include any piece in this book if I didn't think it was good. And I've already told you I like all three of these essays. But if expository writing is all about showing what you know, we should probably take a look at how these writers support their ideas.

INTERESTING IDEAS + BELIEVABLE SUPPORT + CONVERSATIONAL STYLE = A SUCCESSFUL ESSAY

The most important quality that defines an essay is the unique perspective of an individual writer. In essays, writers have great freedom to choose any topic and to say whatever they want about it. But as we learned in a previous chapter, with freedom come responsibility.

All types of personal writing suffer from the same weakness: they're personal. If what you have to say is too specific to your life, your readers may not be able to relate it to theirs. By definition there's going to be a gap between your unique vision of the world and the way your readers see things. So how do you close that gap?

- **Ideas just different enough that they make readers think.** To be a successful essayist, you want to present ideas that are closely related to, but not exactly the same as, the ideas your readers currently hold. You want your ideas to be different enough to be interesting, but not so different that you put people off. Without scaring people away, or making them angry, your original angle on things should make readers take note of what you think and challenge them to rethink their own views on the subject.

Miss Margot says

Think about your favorite comedian or cartoon. The storylines are really all the same. Comics talk about stuff that happens to all of us every day, but what makes their stories funny is their slightly different take on those common events. Similarly, every time I turn on a new cartoon, I see stories played out that are the same as cartoon stories when I was a kid (and that was a long time ago). What's new is that the stories are told just a little differently.

- **Supporting details that make readers trust your observations.** If you're presenting ideas that are new to your readers, how will they come to trust that what you say is right? If a writer says, "Growing up is awful!" and everything you know says it's not, why are you going to believe this person? Because the details the writer offers make you believe that the ideas expressed in the essay are valid. To like an essay, readers don't have to agree with the writer's conclusions, but they do have to understand how those conclusions were reached.

- **A voice that feels like a real person talking.** Another part of trusting the writer comes from our sense of how the writer speaks to us as we read. The best essay writers make their readers feel like they're talking to them, one on one, as part of a conversation. This isn't a big speech to 500 people; it's just talk, plain and simple, between a couple of good friends. There's no secret technique. Just write as though you were talking to someone you know very well.

There's certainly more to creating a successful essay than interesting ideas, strong support, and a conversational style. But I think they represent the most important elements. Of those three, perhaps the most important is how writers show what they know with strong supporting details. Let's look at how that works in each of our three example essays.

STICKING TO THE FACTS

If I want you to understand that not being able find a stick of gum is driving me crazy, how do I do that? Just saying it that way makes it seem stupid, doesn't it? But in "The Last Stick of Gum," the author gives us something we can understand and relate to.

He starts with an experience he knows we've all had: asking someone for gum and having them say they don't have any. Then he gradually pushes the boundary until he's exaggerating so much we know that what he's talking about couldn't possibly happen. And yet, we want to believe it.

The key for me in this essay is the quality of the detail in the third paragraph:

> But soon we see the method in their madness. Our problem seems small at first: we can't seem to focus in class; we miss the winning shot at 3-on-3; we lose a homework assignment and even forget to lie about it. Then it hits us: we want gum. We need gum. We have to have gum.

I've certainly known many kids who couldn't focus in class, who've had bad games in sports, and who've lost their homework. These are real things that really happen. Of course, they never happen because kids don't have enough gum to eat. Or do they? I guess I never really thought about it. And that's exactly what an essayist wants: to get readers thinking about something they've never thought about before.

FORWARD THINKING

In "What Do I Have to Look Forward To?," the author has an unusual view of growing up. But after we've read the piece, it doesn't seem so unusual, does it? Most interesting of all are the writer's perceptions of adults:

> And other adults don't seem much happier either. My friends' parents seem to have just as many problems to deal with. Whenever I visit after school, the moms look tired, and you can forget about even talking to the dads for a couple of hours after they get home from work, if they even get home at all. (In fact, I don't think I've ever met the fathers of some of my friends. It's as though they don't even exist.)

Is this true and accurate? I don't think so. But I have to admit I never gave it much thought until the writer of this essay forced me to think about it. Looking at my own life, I can see how a teenager who observed me, especially after a long day of work, might get the impression that I wasn't very happy. Working in education can be hard and some days I'm grumpy about it.

Wow, what do you know? It happened again: an essayist asked me to consider his vision of life, helped me understand it better by providing details, and then got me to question my own way of looking at things. When I was a kid, I had my fears about growing up, too. But I didn't associate that with the adults around me. Now I'm wondering what kids in school think when they interact with me.

This is the effect a good essay can have on a reader. It's also why the essay is such a powerful and popular form of writing. It's probably the best way to promote a big idea with a small number of words.

GROWING UP IN A HURRY

In the last two essays, the writers used their own observations of life to show what they know. In "When I Grow Up," the writer lets us observe:

> I screamed and sat bolt upright in bed. I gasped swallowing huge amounts of air. I'd just had the most horrible nightmare ever. I'd never been so scared in my life.
>
> Still gasping, I called "Mom!"
>
> My mom came sleepily into my bedroom and sat on the edge of my bed. "What is it, sweetie?" she asked, her voice full of concern.
>
> Tears welled up in my eyes as I remembered the ghostly monster from my dream. "I… I had a nightmare," I finally managed to say.
>
> "Poor thing," my mom said sympathetically as she gave me a hug. "But don't worry," she added. "You will stop having them when you grow up."

This is a classic technique in an expository essay: starting out with a little story, or *anecdote* as it's called, that helps the writer make an important point. Using an anecdote can be very effective. As I mentioned, it lets the reader do the observing and encourages us to draw our own conclusions. It's also nice to get a break from all the explaining the writer will be doing later on. Best of all is the simple fact that everyone seems to love a good story.

I don't know whether the story the writer is telling really happened. But I don't think that matters for the success of this essay. As I mentioned before, we don't have to agree with everything the writer says. We just have to understand it. This little story, made up or not, is a perfect description that does a great job of introducing the writer's point. It may not be real, but it's full of details that make it seem real enough for us to trust what the writer is saying.

CHAPTER NINE

Be an Editorial Writer

TEN THINGS YOU NEED TO KNOW
EVEN IF YOU DON'T READ THIS CHAPTER

1. Editorial writing is a time-honored community tradition that often inspires writers to do their best work.

2. Because everyone has strong opinions about things, editorial writing is usually full of strong feelings. That's what makes it fun to write and fun to read as well.

3. People write editorials to convince other people to change things, or to leave things just the way they are.

4. When we write an editorial, we can't count on being able to convince people of anything. But we can always do our best to shape the debate.

5. Sometimes writers take on big issues that everyone in a community is familiar with. But editorials also give writers an opportunity to bring up things that are not well known or often talked about.

6. It's hard to change a person's mind through a single reading of an editorial because the beliefs we hold are often linked to many other beliefs in a complex system.

7. Because people are so hard to convince, it's better to think about writing editorials as a way of connecting with those who already share your opinions.

8. The potential power of an editorial lies not in changing one person's mind but in pulling together a large of group of people to support a particular point of view.

9. Most of us think it's the logic of an editorial that gets people to agree with it, but it's really the way people feel about the writer that makes the biggest difference.

10. Logic helps readers understand your position, but it takes passion, honesty, and empathy to help them change their minds.

EVERYONE'S ENTITLED TO YOUR OPINION

Live on this planet a while and pretty soon you start feeling one way or another about things. Some things you like; others you don't. Some you want to change; others you're happy with just the way they are. Either way, your mind is made up; you've got your story and you're sticking to it. So why not use a little of that natural human stubbornness to get some good writing done?

Your local newspaper devotes an entire section to people writing about their opinions every day. Called the Opinion and Editorial page, or the Op-Ed page for short, this part of the paper typically features at least one piece written by someone from the newspaper and at least one other piece written by a member of the community. Sometimes everyone in the section writes about the same thing; sometimes they write about different things. Either way, the Op-Ed page is always interesting to read because it's the one spot in the paper where you can be sure people are telling you what they really think.

A RARE OPPORTUNITY

There are few opportunities in life where we get to share our opinions without being interrupted by people who disagree with us. Editorial writing is one of those opportunities. Over the years, working with kids in school, I've discovered that the days we spend writing editorials are some of the best days we have.

I think this is because editorial writing is always full of strong feelings. We all take our opinions very seriously, so it makes sense that when we put them down on paper, we would take our writing seriously, too. For much the same reason, when we read we pay close attention to the opinions of other writers as well.

The stakes are high when we write editorials and that means we usually put in more effort to produce our best work. I know that's certainly true for me. I recently had an editorial published by the biggest paper in our state. At only 750 words, it barely took me an hour to write a first draft. But I must have revised it half a dozen times before I felt comfortable sending it in.

WHY WRITE AN EDITORIAL?

People write editorials for many different reasons. But one of the most common comes up when something in someone's life is about to change in a negative way. In the piece below, an editorial written by a fifth grader for his school newspaper, the writer is concerned about losing recess. Many schools across the country have been trying to cram more learning time into the school day. One way to do that is to take away recess. This writer thinks that would be a bad idea and he wants everyone in his school to know about it.

EXAMPLE:

Don't Take Away Our Recess

The average student spends most of the day in class doing work. But children, as we all know, have trouble sitting for long periods of time, and as the school day is over six hours long, they need more than just a lunch break in the middle. This is only one of many reasons why recess was created. How could anyone even consider taking away one of the greatest ideas ever invented?

Recess was meant to help kids release their energy so they would come back to the classroom ready to learn. But how will that happen when they get rid of both our morning and afternoon breaks? If they take away even one recess children may be too energetic and hyper to pay attention to their lessons. There will be more disruptions. Talking in class will increase. The fine art of passing notes will reach a new level. Who knows? Kids may learn even less without recess.

Before we make such a big change to our school's schedule, we should think carefully about it. Morning and afternoon recess have been a tradition as far back as anybody can remember. I asked our student teacher, Ms. Roberts, about it (she went to third, fourth, and fifth grade here when she was our age) and she said she always got two recesses. How can we do away with something that so many people have depended on for so many years?

It's not just a matter of education. Lots of parents agree that children should enjoy their youth while they can and live a worry-free life before they face the real world. After all, you have to admit, being cramped up in a desk all day is rather uncomfortable, not to mentionh boring at times. So, not only do kids need recess to learn, they need it to maintain their youth.

As you've probably heard, lots of kids are complaining about too much homework lately. This is the main reason that some people want to take away recess, to cover the homework during this time. But most schools have only a fifteen-minute recess in the morning and another one in the afternoon. How much learning can you pack into that little amount of time anyway? Recess isn't long enough for heavy duty studying; it's just enough time for kids to get their energy out.

What would school be like without recess? I don't even want to think about it. Right now, losing a recess is a punishment you can get if you get in trouble. Not having any recesses would make us feel like we were being punished every day. Think back to when you were a kid. I'll bet you got two recesses. How would you have felt if they had been taken away?

There are several things I like about this piece. First of all, I like the idea that a kid wrote it. Most of the time, kids are left out of changes in school policies that affect them. This time, a student's voice is heard. Regardless of how the issue is resolved, I think it's great that a student spoke up for what he believed in. That's what editorial writing is all about.

At certain points in the piece, I think the author is being a bit silly. The art of note passing probably isn't going rise to the level where it begins to ruin class time. And it's hard to imagine kids needing recess to maintain their youth. But right at the end, when the writer asks his audience to remember back to when they were kids in school, I think he's found a strong emotional hook that will get the attention of the people he wants to influence.

YOUR OWN ISSUES

The issues we write about in editorials are often those that affect many people: a law about to be passed, a policy about to be changed, an election about to be held. But sometimes we push issues of our own, things we think are important, even though the rest of our community might not even know about them.

In this next example, a high school junior speaks out on an issue most of us probably never think about. As kids get to the end of high school, many get part-time jobs. For most of us, this seems like a normal part of growing up. But this writer thinks differently and has chosen to write an editorial to get her point across.

EXAMPLE:

Teenagers Need Educations, Not Jobs

Education is a key element in developing the skills necessary for a successful life. But many students put more energy into earning a paycheck than they put into earning A's. Students need to realize that their high school classes can prepare them for a brighter future—but only if they work hard to do well in the present.

A high school student's schedule can be packed from the time they wake up to the time they go to bed. There's the school day, of course, plus extracurricular activities. Add a job into this busy schedule and there's little time to devote to academics. Kids with jobs may get lower grades or take less challenging courses. Jobs also limit the amount of time students have for social activities and sports. This can mean a withdrawal from friends and the school community.

If the jobs high school students could get were more beneficial, there might be more reasons for kids to have them. But in most cases, the wages are low, the hours are long, and the work isn't something that helps them build important skills for the future.

Worst of all is the lure of a regular paycheck. Six or seven dollars an hour can seem like a lot to a student in high school. Some may become comfortable with this and not strive to reach their full potential.

Money is the root of many problems associated with teenagers. A paycheck gives students the power to buy things they want like clothes, a car, or electronics. But it also gives them the power to buy other things like drugs and alcohol. For some working students, managing money can be a challenge. So even those who work hard and do well on the job may face unexpected problems.

Teenagers already have enough stress in their lives. A job just makes things worse. Teenagers also struggle to manage their time wisely. How can we expect most of them to successfully juggle academics along with a work schedule? High school is a time when teenagers should be preparing for their futures. Students should focus their attention on their studies so they can one day achieve their dreams.

Though I'm around working high school students all the time, I had never even considered this issue until I read this piece. I'm still not sure what I think about it, but at least this writer got me thinking. I had a part-time job during my senior year of high school, and I worked for at least part of every school year when I was in college. I really felt like I needed the money, but I can also remember being tired during the day, losing my weekends and nights to work, and never feeling like I was doing quite enough to keep up with school. When I think about how little money I made working part-time for scarcely more than minimum wage, I wonder now if it was worth it.

The editorials you choose to write don't have to address the most popular issues of the day. Sometimes the best editorial writers are those who call attention to issues no one ever thinks about. Each of us sees things a little differently. How you look at the world and what you think is important deserve to be considered. But people can't consider what they don't know about or understand. That's why newspapers have traditionally offered this forum to their readers. Everyone in a community, even regular folks like you and me, deserves to have a voice. Editorial writing is a great way to use it.

Miss Margot says

When I was in high school, I wrote an editorial for the school paper on the poor attendance at our annual charity dance marathon. I was kind of mad that more people didn't come out to support the event, and I talked a lot about student apathy and selfishness. Some people at my school got mad; others didn't even know there had been a dance marathon. My teacher liked the editorial so much, she entered it in a statewide student journalism contest and it was one of the top finishers. So, any topic is a good one as long as you're passionate about it and have something important to say.

THE TRUE POWER OF PERSUASIVE WRITING

When we write editorials, we don't have to change the world, but we do have to change our readers' minds. In school we would say that editorial writing is persuasive writing. In persuasive writing, we create an argument to convince people that our way of looking at things is right and that other ways are wrong.

This is not easy. In fact, it's almost impossible.

In most cases, human beings form their beliefs over long periods of time. It can take weeks, months, or even years to build a belief and just as long to change it. This is because any single belief we hold is likely to be connected to or made up of many other beliefs as well. As a result, getting people to change their minds about one thing often involves getting them to change their minds about many things. A few hundred words—even well written ones—are often no match for the complex system of pre-existing ideas readers have inside their heads.

So why bother?

That's a good question. As someone who spends most of his writing life trying to change the way people think about things, I can tell you why I bother. There are things I care about deeply, mostly things about kids and school. I have strong feelings about the way I want education to be. But education is such a big thing I can't do much about it all by myself. To make progress toward my vision of education in our country, I need other people to care about the same things I do. Putting my opinions down in words—and having my writing appear in newspapers, magazines, on the web, anywhere—helps me find others who believe the same things I do.

Remember that editorial I just wrote? Half a dozen friends told me how much they liked it. And three more people I've never even met before wrote to congratulate me as well. That's nine people I can now count as sharing my beliefs about a particular issue, nine people I might be able to ask in the future to help me achieve my goals. This is why I attempt to persuade people through writing: I'm hoping to find others who believe the same things I do.

WRITE TO CONNECT, NOT TO CONVINCE

Even though editorial writing is considered persuasive writing, it's difficult to imagine that any writing could truly persuade a reader of anything—unless they already believed it. This is why I think of editorial writing not as writing to convince but as writing to connect.

Take our fifth grader trying to save recess. Do you really think the principal of his school is going change the policy because one eleven-year-old kid says he should? Not likely. But if kids all over the school read the editorial and tell their parents about it, and if a group of parents gets a group of teachers together, and if fifty kids, twenty parents, and ten teachers go to the principal to save recess, there's a chance that our enterprising young editorial writer might get his way.

That's how editorial writing works. When we write to convince, we're really writing to connect with other people in our community who already believe the same things we do. Our writing is a catalyst that calls this group together, energizes the people within it to move in a specific direction, and multiplies the effectiveness of our lone voice. This is the true power of persuasive writing. It's the power to bring like-minded people together to support you and your ideas about the way things should be.

BE A WRITER LIKE PETER SPRUYT

Peter Spruyt is a Los Angeles-based writer, actor, and stand-up comedian. He has created two original television pilots and a screenplay about Internet dating. He has been featured as an actor and stand-up comic in several movies and television shows, including Men In Black II, Jimmy Kimmel Live, My Name Is Earl *and Comedy Central's* Premium Blend.

WHAT KIND OF WRITER ARE YOU?

I write screenplays and stand-up comedy. I am a professional stand-up comedian, and I write all my own jokes.

WHY DO YOU WRITE?

I write because it's fun! I enjoy writing funny jokes and stories. When other people laugh after hearing my jokes or reading my stories, it gives me a great feeling of satisfaction.

WHAT MADE YOU WANT TO BE A WRITER?

When I was young, I read great books and watched funny movies, and I admired the talents of the people who wrote them. It made me want to create works of my own that people could enjoy.

Q

A

WHAT ADVICE WOULD YOU GIVE TO A FELLOW WRITER WHO WAS JUST STARTING OUT?

Write! Writing is like playing a sport or a musical instrument: the more you write, the better you become.

Let people read what you write, and see what they think. Pay attention to the notes you get from your teachers. Try to keep doing the things they like and improving on the things they don't.

Read! There are so many great writers you can learn from. If you like certain writers, try to figure out what they do that makes their writing appealing and try to emulate them.

Create your own style! What makes you unique? Do you have experiences or a point of view that makes you different from other people? Try to incorporate the things that make you different and special into your writing.

Good luck. Have fun!

THE SECRET OF SUCCESSFUL PERSUASIVE WRITING

Most people think you have to be good at coming up with logical arguments to be a good persuasive writer. But I've got a secret for you: there's something more important than that.

It's true that logical thinking plays an important role in a successful editorial. In particular, we have to offer strong supporting details to help our readers understand our conclusions. For example, our fifth grader offered these reasons why two daily recesses should be saved:

- Recess helps kids release energy so they can concentrate in class.

- Taking away recess would increase disruptions.

- Recess is necessary for helping kids enjoy their youth.

- Recess has been a tradition at this elementary school for a long time.

- Kids would feel punished if they lost their recess.

Our high schooler, concerned about her classmates putting more effort into their jobs than their studies, also had good support for her opinion:

- Doing well in school is more important to kids' futures than the small amount of money they can make from a job.

- High school kids already have stressful schedules; a job makes this worse.

- Having a job limits the contact kids have with their friends and their school.

- Kids sometimes use the money they make to buy alcohol and drugs.
- Feeling successful in a low-wage job could discourage kids from trying for something better.

Both writers did a fine job of telling us why they think what they think. But can logic alone move us to support their positions? Probably not. Personally, I liked their pieces, but I'm not sure I would agree with what they said even if I agreed it made sense. Truth is, readers aren't always logical. Nobody is. As human beings, we all hold illogical beliefs and do illogical things. Why? Because we feel like it.

FEELINGS COME FIRST

How many times have your parents or your teachers told you to do something you knew was the right thing to do and yet you still didn't do it? This happens all the time. As an adult, I'm even more aware of it in my life now than when I was a kid.

I know the kinds of food I should eat, but do I eat that way? Not even close. And I won't even try to lie to you about it. Last night, for example, I had a big, thick hamburger with a huge pile of greasy fries and three Cokes. I also had a delicious fried empanada with guacamole. And I didn't stop there. Late at night—and this is really bad—I had two cookies, one peanut butter and one chocolate chip. I know all the logical arguments for maintaining a good diet. I also know that I'm about thirty pounds overweight and that my cholesterol is too high. And yet I consciously chose last night to ignore all of this logic simply because I felt like it. I could read a hundred persuasive pieces on the importance of eating right and I'd still eat wrong on a regular basis.

TIP:

Never forget that your audience is made up of regular human beings just like you. And for most regular human beings, feelings trump logic every time. Old habits die hard, and that goes for habits of mind, too. This doesn't mean being logical in your writing is pointless. But it does mean you can't count on logic alone to move people toward your way of looking at things.

IS IT THE WRITING OR THE WRITER?

Has this ever happened to you? You spend weeks trying to convince someone of something, but you just can't. In fact, the harder you try, the more they end up dead set against you. Then one day, all of a sudden it seems, you hear them say exactly the same thing you've been saying. When you ask them why they now agree with you, however, they credit someone else with giving them the information they really needed.

This can be incredibly frustrating, but it's also incredibly common. There's nothing worse for most of us than being ignored. And that's exactly what it feels like when someone we care about rejects what we've been telling them for months and then, in a heartbeat, takes exactly the same advice from someone else. Why does this happen? Because often it's not the right idea people are waiting for, it's the right person with the right idea.

When someone tries to convince us of something, and we end up being convinced, it's as though we are agreeing to follow them as they lead us into something new. This is scary, so we tend to follow people we feel most comfortable with. When it comes to editorials and other persuasive communication, it turns out people are often persuaded more by the writer than they are by the writing.

In life, our sense of comfort with a particular person is determined by many factors, most having to do with how we've gotten along with them in the past. In writing, however, we usually don't have past interactions with our readers. So what do our readers need to feel comfortable with us as we attempt to lead them in a new direction?

Trust. In order for readers to follow us, they have to feel like they can trust us. In persuasive writing, I have learned that readers are more likely to trust writers if they find three things in their writing:

- **Passion.** Can you tell that the writer really cares about his or her position? If someone is going to follow you, they want to know you care deeply about your ideas and that you will remain committed to them even if things get hard. Part of the meaning of the word "passion" is "suffering." Readers sometimes need to know you have suffered for your cause or that other people you care about have suffered. They also want to know you're clear enough about what you're fighting for to know why you're fighting for it.

- **Honesty.** Is the writer telling us the truth? Trust is based, first and foremost, on honesty. But it's hard to convince someone you're being honest through writing. After all, you can't just say, "I'm honest! Trust me!" That'll probably produce the reverse of what you're looking for. But you can keep your language simple and your logic clear. It's human nature to distrust people who use fancy words, even when we know what those fancy words mean.

TIP:

People who use simple language are generally judged to be more trustworthy than those who don't. Simple logic is also appealing. Don't pile on tons and tons of evidence. That makes people think you're trying too hard to convince them. Stick with two or three points at most and focus on those that are likely to elicit a strong emotional response in addition to their logical appeal.

- **Empathy.** Does the writer understand how other people feel who are connected to this issue? Persuasive writing is all about change; we're always asking people to change things or to keep things from changing. Change is hard; for some people it's downright scary. In order to trust you, readers want to know that you understand how hard or how scary it might be for them to make the change you're asking them to make. They may also want to know if you have any ideas for making things easier or less scary if they decide to support you in making this change happen.

Over the years, I've come to believe that when I write an editorial or other persuasive piece, I'm not asking my readers to support my ideas; I'm asking them to support me personally. Supporting a person is more of an emotional decision than it is an intellectual decision. I certainly have to be logical and clear; that's the only way people will understand the change I am asking them to make. But even if my readers understand me, they still may not believe me. That's where I need to show my passion, honesty, and empathy, because in order to change my readers' minds, I first have to change their hearts.

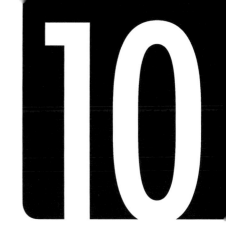

CHAPTER TEN

Be a Fiction Writer

TEN THINGS YOU NEED TO KNOW
EVEN IF YOU DON'T READ THIS CHAPTER

1. Fiction is the hardest genre to write because it's so challenging to come up with a story that is both believable and entertaining.

2. Starting a fiction story can be easy because you can write just about anything you want, but continuing past a certain point gets very hard, and coming up with a good ending can seem almost impossible.

3. Using the Five Facts of Fiction makes fiction writing easier because it provides a solid framework for creating a story that you can refer to throughout the writing process.

4. The key to writing great stories is to have great characters.

5. It takes a lot of information to create great characters and that means taking time before writing to figure out as many things as you can about who your characters are.

6. If characters didn't want things, they wouldn't do things, and stories would be boring. Knowing what your characters want is vital to creating an interesting plot.

7. The plot is not really made up from scratch. It comes from who your characters are and what your characters want.

8. As a result of trying to get what they want, your characters are changed in some way. This can be the most meaningful part of your story.

9. Think of the setting not as place and time but as an entire world you create just for your story.

10. Though it certainly isn't required, working out a detailed Five Facts of Fiction is a great thing to do before you begin your story.

THE HARDEST THING TO WRITE

If you've been reading this book from the beginning, you've probably noticed by now that certain messages keep popping up over and over. Perhaps the most common one is this: it's hard to be a writer. Writing every day is hard. Facing a blank page is hard. Getting your punctuation right is hard. Revising is really hard.

But of all the hard things writers do to be writers, writing fiction is probably the hardest of all—at least in my opinion.

Now don't go disagreeing with me right away. Stick around for a few pages and hear me out. I know that most of the students I work with love to write fiction and that they consider fiction to be much easier than some of the other types of writing I make them do. But that's only how they feel at first.

Most of us start out thinking of fiction as just some kind of made-up story. This makes it seem easy because we think we can write anything we want. Then we start writing. At first, ideas come quickly: this happens, then that happens, then this happens, then that happens. Before we know it, we've got a story going. But as soon as someone else reads it, we encounter the cold, hard truth: it *is* easy to write a made-up story, but almost impossible to write a good one.

Miss Margot says

People are always telling me I'm a really good writer (which is a good thing since that's how I make a living), but they've never seen my fiction writing. I don't think it's nearly as good as the other stuff I write. But I still write it—just for fun—because I like trying to make it as good as the books I read.

FICTION AND ME

The way I feel about fiction writing comes from my own experience with it, of course. I've never been able to do it well. I've tried many times, but have never come up with something I liked. No matter what I write or how I write it, my stories never seem believable. I've also found it difficult to finish a story once I've started it. Endings are hard enough in other kinds of writing; in fiction, coming up with a good ending seems to me like solving an impossible puzzle.

I've also taught fiction writing many times and watched how students struggle with it. Starting a story seems easy enough, but with each page a writer adds, more problems pop up: Why would the main character do that? What happened to the character you introduced two pages ago? How does the scene you just wrote go with the other scenes in your story? It seems like the kids I work with have many of the same problems I do. Then again, according to the research I've done on writing fiction, the best professional writers struggle with these things, too.

INVENTING THE TRUTH

Ironically, the thing about fiction that makes us think it will be easy is the thing that makes it hard. Yes, the story is made up. And yes, we can make up anything we want—but only at the beginning. As soon as we set down the basic elements, everything that comes afterward has to fit with what has come before in a way the reader will find believable.

A work of fiction isn't true, but it has to seem to the reader as though it could be. This means fiction writers have to invent the truth of their stories from scratch. Think about how much harder this is than writing a memoir, for example. In a memoir, any time you get stuck or need more detail, all you have to do is think about what happened to you.

You don't have to create anything; you just have to remember it. But when you get stuck writing fiction, there's nothing to remember; you have to make up something new from scratch.

TIP:

It turns out that recounting the truth is a lot easier than inventing it. And that's why I recommend that writers work with memoir for a while before they work with fiction. Real life provides us with a framework we can rely on to make good decisions about what to write next. With fiction, this framework has to be supplied by the writer.

FINDING A FRAMEWORK FOR FICTION

When I was a kid in school, the stories I wrote featured boring characters, ridiculous plots, and contrived endings. Even if I had a good idea to start with, I didn't know how to develop it. The more I wrote, the worse my stories became.

The problem was that I never took time to think about my stories before I wrote them. I just started in before I knew much about my characters or their situations. Now, when I teach fiction writing, I help kids solve this problem by introducing them to The Five Facts of Fiction:

- **Fact #1: Fiction is all about character.** A good story starts with a good character. Writers need to know a lot about their characters before they begin. Too many young writers start first with the plot. I think that's backwards. We can write a better story if we first create a main character and let the plot develop based on who our character is.

- **Fact #2: Fiction is all about what your character wants.** If characters didn't want things, they wouldn't do things to try to get them. Try to imagine one thing your character wants more than anything else in the world. The more important this thing is to your character, the more he or she will do to get it. Your character's motivation inspires your story's plot.

- **Fact #3: Fiction is all about how your character gets or does not get what he or she wants.** This is the plot, the sequence of events that propels your readers from beginning to end. By looking at this issue third, after knowing your character and your character's motivation, you can create events in your story that make sense and seem naturally suited to your character and his or her situation.

- **Fact #4: Fiction is all about how your character changes.** Your character wants something very important. Your character does things to try and get it. Stuff happens along the way. Maybe your character gets it, maybe not. Either way, your character is changed by the experience. This is where much of the meaning in your story comes from.

- **Fact #5: Fiction is all about a world you create.** Your character probably wouldn't do much if he or she didn't have a place to do it in, other people to do it with, or a time period to be a part of. Every story takes place in its own unique world. You have to create that world from scratch.

Early on in the process of teaching fiction writing to kids, I learned an important lesson: before we could write good stories, we needed to pre-write them. Pre-writing is something I encourage writers to do no matter what kind of writing they're trying to produce. But with fiction, I consider it a requirement.

The Five Facts of Fiction isn't the only way to sketch out a story. In fact, there are dozens of ways, many created by famous professionals. But I like Five Facts best. It's the only thing I've come across that has helped me break through my fiction writer's block. And I know it has helped many students I've worked with, too.

A CHARACTER YOU CARE ABOUT

Fact of Fiction #1 says that fiction is all about character. When you think about a story, think about a character first. Great fiction is driven by great characters. An interesting plot and a well described setting are important. But having great characters is the most important thing of all. So what makes a character great?

It's never easy to answer questions like this. There are so many different kinds of characters and so many reasons why we find them compelling. If we asked fifty readers and fifty writers what they thought, we'd probably get a hundred different answers. But I'll bet each one of those hundred people would agree with this statement: a great character is a character you care about.

Reading a story is like watching someone's life without being able to interact with them. All you can do is cheer from the sidelines when things go their way or worry about them when things go badly. But you can't cheer or worry if you don't care to begin with.

So that leads to the next obvious question: How do we make characters our readers will care about? Fortunately, I think this one has an answer that's a little easier to tease out. In order for a reader to care about a character, the reader has to identify with or relate to the character in some way.

When we identify with a character, it means we think the character is like us. In the best situations, we think the character is a lot like us, maybe even exactly like us. As we follow them through the story, we develop the sense that what happens to them is in some way happening to us, too, and this is what makes us want to keep reading.

Relating to a character is a little different. In this case, the character might not be very much like us at all, but we still feel connected for some reason. Maybe we know someone who is like the character. Or maybe we understand certain things about the character's situation.

Or, best of all, even though the character is completely different from us in just about every way, we know exactly how the character feels when good or bad things happen.

Unfortunately, as a writer, there's no way to know ahead of time if your readers will care about your character. So you might as well start with a character you care about and see what happens from there.

A CHARACTER I CARE ABOUT

A while back, I came up with a character named Damon. The more I've worked with him, the more I've come to feel I might have a good one. I made him up one day while I was teaching The Five Facts of Fiction to a group of eighth graders. To give my audience the best chance of connecting with Damon, I started out by making him an eighth grader, too. Actually, he just finished eighth grade and is about to go to high school. So my first instinct in coming up with a character was to choose one that was just about the same age as my audience.

> Damon is fourteen and about to enter ninth grade. He lives in Texas. He's grown up in the city all his life but recently moved to a nearby suburb with his mom and little brother because his parents got divorced. He's big, stocky, and muscular, but also quick and coordinated. He loves football and is one of the few players who can "go both ways", meaning that he can play both offense and defense. On offense he's a fullback, but defense is really his specialty. He plays defensive line and is so strong and so quick that no one can stop him. His coach last year gave him the nickname "Texas Hold 'Em" because he's as big as Texas and he can hold the line all by himself.
>
> Damon is angry and confused. His parents' divorce was a surprise to him. He knew his mom didn't like it when his dad had to travel so much for his business, but his dad always seemed to make plenty of money and the family always seemed to have a good life. Their condo in the city was small—only two bedrooms—but he didn't mind sharing a room with his little brother. He liked the neighborhood and the friends he had there.

Damon lives now in a beautiful house in the suburbs. He has his own bedroom, and it's huge. He has a brand new computer for school. And he got more new clothes this year than ever. His mom also got him his own TV and a subscription to all the NFL games on cable. But none of these things can make up for how upset he is about his family. He doesn't even feel like playing football this year and is considering not going out for his high school team, even though he's certain to be a star and the coach has already called his house to encourage him.

Damon is an introvert. To some people he seems shy. He's quiet and doesn't say much unless you ask him a question. But inside he's always thinking carefully about things. But now, when he should be thinking about enjoying the end of his summer and getting ready for his first season of high school football, he's brooding about his family life and wondering if there wasn't something wrong all those years. When he thinks about it, his family was unusual. His mom worked at home on a computer doing all kinds of different projects and his dad would some-times leave for several weeks at a time for his business. Damon never knew exactly what he did but it never mattered much. Life always seemed good to Damon and he always thought everything was fine. Now he doesn't know what to think about anything.

So that's Damon. What do you think of him? It's probably too early to tell. Most readers need a fair amount of information to connect strongly with a character. And I'm planning to give you that informa-tion as I work through the rest of the Five Facts of Fiction. As you learn more about Damon, I hope he'll become a character you care about.

A REASON FOR DOING SOMETHING

Imagine this: Damon doesn't want to play football. Damon doesn't like his new friends. Damon doesn't want to go to his new school. So when the first day of class rolls around, what does Damon do? Nothing. He just stays in bed. Next morning, same thing. And so it goes, day after day.

How interesting will this story be?

The problem is that Damon doesn't want anything. Characters who don't want anything don't do anything. And a story about a character who doesn't do anything probably won't be very interesting. Fact of Fiction #2 says that fiction is all about what our character wants. If our character wants nothing, our story goes nowhere.

To make our story go, we need to make our character go. To do that, we need to know what our character wants and why he wants it. Whatever this is, it has to be something very important to our character, something he cares about so much he's willing to go to great lengths to get it.

So what's going to get Damon out of bed? School? He doesn't want to go to his new school. Football? He doesn't think he wants to play anymore. Friends? All his friends are back in the city where he used to live. So what will it be?

> Damon wants to live with his dad back in the city. He doesn't know exactly where his dad lives now, but he knows he has a small apartment within a few miles of where they used to live. Damon sees the situation like this: if his family has to be split up, his mom can have his little brother and he'll go live with his dad. That way, he can be back in the city with his friends and go to the same high school he'd always been planning to go to.
>
> But there's more to this than just a neighborhood to live in and a place to go to school. For the first time in his life, Damon feels a little unsure of himself. Football in Texas is very serious. And high school football is as serious as it gets. Damon knows he's an unusually talented player and he's heard his coaches hint at the possibility of a big-time college or even pro career. He didn't realize it in the spring, but now, at the end of the summer, the start of high school has felt like the start of something bigger than Damon is ready for, especially if his dad won't be around.

His dad was always the one who encouraged him to play, who got him through tough times like when he was injured two years ago, and who helped him become the great player that he is.

Finally, Damon misses his dad. Just before he and his mom and his brother moved to the new house, his dad left on another one of his business trips. But this time he was gone for several months, much longer than usual. Damon knows he just returned because he got a postcard in the mail. Thinking of his dad coming back to the city makes him feel like he should be back there, too.

Now we've got something. Specifically, we've got a problem for our character to solve. Separated from his father and the friends he's grown up with, facing a year at a school he doesn't like, confused about his ambitions to be a football star, Damon has to take action. Staying in bed all day doing nothing isn't an option.

So what does Damon decide to do? That's how the plot of our story takes shape. Fact of Fiction #1 tells us who our character is. Fact of Fiction #2 tells us what our character wants. Fact of Fiction #3 tells us how our character goes about getting it.

BE A WRITER LIKE MICAELA ARNESON

Micaela Arneson is an eighth grade student who writes not only for class assignments, but also for fun. Her favorite genre of writing is fiction, but she has had experience writing essays, book reviews, research papers, newspaper articles, presentations, and science reports.

WHAT KIND OF WRITER ARE YOU?

I am a student writer. Most of my pieces are for class assignments, but in my free time (which I don't have much of) I write fictional stories.

WHY DO YOU WRITE?

In the classroom, I write for a grade. But when I'm at home writing stories, I write for myself. I write so I can get my thoughts organized and then share those thoughts with others. And last, but definitely not least, I write because I enjoy it. For me, writing is fun!

WHAT MADE YOU WANT TO BE A WRITER?

I've always wanted to be a writer because I've had positive experiences with all kinds of literature. When I was in kindergarten, my friends and I would sit together during "Literary Time" and discuss topics for our newest piece of writing. We authored and illustrated many "books", and I looked forward to that time every day. I also loved, and still love, to read. I enjoy reading any genre, and I believe that a lot of what has contributed to my love of writing is my love of reading.

Q

WHAT ADVICE WOULD YOU GIVE TO A FELLOW WRITER WHO WAS JUST STARTING OUT?

A

Write as often and as much as you can. As the saying goes, "Practice makes perfect," and I think that's very true, especially in writing. Write down your observations, feelings, dreams, whatever you feel like. Experiment with different types of writing. Set goals for yourself and exercise areas that need work. Maybe you don't have enough description in your writing. To fix that, you could pick out everyday objects and write down everything you observe about them. Describe how things look, feel, sound, maybe even taste. Work as hard as you can and don't ever be afraid to keep going.

WHAT HAPPENS NEXT?

If I've got a good story going here, you'll be eager to find out what happens next. That's the trick to keeping readers reading. Each time something happens in the story, I want you to wonder what's going to happen after that. And I want you to keep wondering all the way to the end.

The sequence of events that makes up a story is called the plot. Fact of Fiction #3 says that fiction is all about how a character gets or does not get what he or she wants. This is how the plot takes shape.

Because he wants something, Damon is going to do something to get it. Every time he does something, something else will happen. As a result, he'll either be closer to or farther from his goal. And then he'll have to think of something else to do. The moment he decides what he wants and gets up out of bed to try and get it, Damon puts himself on a path. That path is the plot of the story.

> As Damon peers out his bedroom window on the first day of school, he sees kids getting on the school bus. But he also sees adults getting on a city bus across the street. Even though he doesn't know exactly where the city bus goes, he figures it has to go into the city eventually. A half hour later, he's on the city bus by himself hoping to find his way to where his dad is living now.
>
> Damon's trip to see his father is not an easy one. Finding his way out of the suburbs and into the city takes several buses and several hours. Then he has to find his father without an address or phone number to go on. Along the way, Damon meets many unusual people. Some are helpful; some are not. Some make Damon feel afraid, others are strangely comforting to him even though he doesn't know them. At one point, Damon is lost in the city transit yard after midnight. Here he meets the strangest people of all, an entire community living in old railway cars and broken down buses.

> Early in the morning, about an hour before sunrise, Damon finds his dad's apartment. His dad isn't home, so Damon breaks in through a window and sits down in the living room to wait for him. A couple of hours later, when Damon's dad gets home, he's furious. He and Damon argue. Damon wants to live with him. His dad says he can't. Damon asks why. But his dad won't tell him.
>
> In the end, Damon's dad reveals the reason why he and his mother got divorced and explains why Damon can't live with him. This is a secret Damon's dad and mom vowed never to tell their children.

With luck, even here at the very end, the reader will still be wondering what's going to happen next. What is the secret? And what will Damon do when he discovers what it is? This sense of anticipation is what keeps readers reading and enjoying themselves with every turn of the page.

EVERYTHING MUST CHANGE

As the old saying goes, "The only thing constant is change." And so it is with a good story. Fact of Fiction #4 says that fiction is all about how a character changes. Characters go through a lot on the way to getting or not getting what they want. They take serious risks and face huge obstacles. It's hard work being a character: the hours are long, the pay is low, and the retirement benefits aren't what they used to be. Worst of all, there's no guarantee that everything a character struggles for will materialize. An experience like this is bound to change a person.

TIP:

Characters are a certain way when we create them. As we take them on their journey, they change. They change in obvious ways, like getting older or living in different places (sometimes they even die). But they change in not-so-obvious ways, too, ways that involve understanding more about who they are as people and what they believe about life. It's these kinds of changes readers tend to be most interested in.

HOW DAMON CHANGES

In the process of trying to find his dad, Damon takes a literal journey from the suburbs into the city. He also takes a journey within himself. He thinks he's looking for his father, but he's really looking for answers to questions he has had all his life.

> In the beginning, Damon is angry, confused, resentful, scared, even a little depressed. His world has just been turned upside down. His family is different. He has a new place to live. He has a new school, new friends, a whole new life. And nobody ever asked him what he thought about any of this; it just happened.
>
> In the end, even though Damon doesn't get to live with his dad, he feels somehow relieved. Learning the secret that led to his parents' divorce and the reason why his dad can't take care of him seems to make all the changes he's been through over the summer seem okay. He's no longer angry at his parents, or confused or resentful. He understands now that they were just doing the best they could and that they made the choices they made out of love for him and his brother, and for each other, too. More than anything, Damon arrives at a feeling of acceptance about the way things are. He'd still like his life to be different, but he knows now that he and his family will be all right no matter what.

It's impossible to change in a significant way like this without learning something at the same time. Sometimes it's something characters learn about themselves, sometimes it's something readers learn about characters, and sometimes it's a little of both. Either way, there's a lesson in this story—maybe even more than one—like the moral at the end of a fable or a fairy tale.

> Damon learns that adult life is a lot more complicated than kid life and that he shouldn't judge adults by his own simplistic kid standards. Life isn't like a football play where all you have to do is charge toward the guy with the ball and bring him down. In fact, life isn't like a game at all. In life, situations come up that just aren't in the play book, and nobody knows the right way to handle them. The best thing we can do is not give up. Keep fighting for what you want, accept defeat with grace and understanding when it presents itself; don't focus on the past and what should have happened; pay attention to the present and what *is* happening.

Though I said earlier that a good character is the most important element of a good story, how that character changes, and what that character learns, may be equally important. The change, and the lesson we learn from it, make the story meaningful. And that's what makes us remember it long after we've turned the last page.

EVERYBODY WANTS TO RULE THE WORLD

It's human nature to get a charge out of being in charge. In the real world, this doesn't happen too often. It seems like there's always someone in charge of us. But in the cozy confines of a story, the author calls the shots and nobody else says otherwise.

With such great power comes great possibility—and a lot of hard work to do. In every moment of every part of your story, some character is interacting with some part of the world in which that story takes place.

Every character exists somewhere, is going somewhere, or is leaving somewhere. And those somewheres have to be accounted for.

The responsibility of creating a world for your story exists even if you choose a realistic setting. Take my story, for example. It's set in Texas, partly in a suburb, partly in an urban area. Since most of us know what those situations are like, you'd think I could just leave it at that and move on. But I can't. Even though Damon's new neighborhood is exactly like many other suburban neighborhoods, it's not other suburban neighborhoods. It's Damon's suburban neighborhood, and I still have to tell my readers exactly what it's like. Same goes when Damon hits the city. It's not just any city, it's the city Damon grew up in and hopes to return to. That makes it special. And when I get to scenes like Damon's night in the transit yard, I have to be even more imaginative.

DAMON'S WORLD

The world of a story includes more than just locations. It also includes people, objects, activities, and even things you can't touch or see like concepts, feelings, ideas, and beliefs. The world of a story can include anything you know from the real world, things from the past, and even—if you're writing science fiction or fantasy—things that don't exist anywhere but your imagination. Admittedly, realistic settings are probably the easiest to work with. And I think that's why all the story ideas I've ever come up with have had settings like the one I've chosen for Damon's world:

> Damon lives in an upper-middle-class suburb just outside a big city in Texas. He lives with his mom and his seven-year-old brother in a house that seems far bigger than what they really need. Everything in Damon's neighborhood looks clean and neat. All the houses are big and white, just like his. It's very quiet at night and not even very noisy during the day because everyone seems to be away somewhere doing something. Nobody just hangs around like they used to when Damon lived in the city.

Everyone seems busy all the time, even though it's summer and there's no school yet. Since he moved in a few weeks ago, Damon has met several of the kids in the neighborhood, sort of, but only as they're coming and going from wherever they come and go to. Damon knows he's different from them and they act like they know it, too.

This place feels strange to Damon though he can't figure out exactly why. It's very nice, much nicer than where he used to live. But something's not quite right. The one thing Damon has noticed from the minute he arrived is how nice everything is. Everyone has a nice house. Everyone drives a nice car. Everyone wears nice clothes, even when they work in the yard. But why does this bother him?

While I think I'm off to a good start here, I obviously have a long way to go. I've told you a bit about the neighborhood, for example, but I haven't described the inside of Damon's house or his room where our story starts. Then there's the city, of course, and Damon's dad's apartment. There are also buses and the transit yard and several other scenes I haven't figured out yet.

Finally, there's my choice of location, in general. I knew the minute I thought of this story that I wanted it to be set in Texas because high school football is such a big deal there. I knew, too, that I would need a suburb and a city. But I didn't want to use any existing cities or suburbs in Texas by name. Instead, I wanted to be free to create my own. I wanted this world to be Damon's world, unique to him and to his story.

JUST ADD WATER

By figuring out the five facts of my fictional story, I've gotten myself to a point where I think I might be ready to start writing—*might* be ready. There's still quite a bit of thinking to be done. But at least I have a start, and I feel like it's a good one.

Using the Five Facts of Fiction strategy doesn't get your story written. In fact, little of what I've written about Damon in this chapter is likely to end up in my story; it's just pre-writing. But it sure feels like good pre-writing. Each of the Five Facts has helped me work out an important part of my piece. And now that I have those parts worked out, I feel like I might have a story worth writing.

You know when you go to the store and you get those little cans of frozen juice and then you pour that goopy stuff into a pitcher and add water to it? Or how about when you make lemonade from a container by taking a scoop of that powder and then putting water in? That's what I think Five Facts of Fiction is like. It's like juice concentrate or lemonade powder. Once you've got your facts worked out, all you have to do is add the water of your imagination and soon you'll have your readers drinking in a great story.

CHAPTER ELEVEN

Be a Book Reviewer

TEN THINGS YOU NEED TO KNOW
EVEN IF YOU DON'T READ THIS CHAPTER

1   Choosing a book to read is a personal process readers take very seriously.

2   Book reviewers help readers make better choices by giving them information and insight they can't get anywhere else.

3   Writing book reviews is one of the most enjoyable kinds of writing you can do in school.

4   Most book reviews contain the same essential elements: the book title, the author's name, a brief summary, the reviewer's favorite parts, and a recommendation.

5   Reviews give you freedom to talk about many different things related to your book.

6   The key to writing a great book review is to concentrate on the things that mattered most to you as you read the book.

7   The best book reviews not only tell us something about the book, they tell us something about the reviewer, too.

8   Most people have never written a book review. But that's just because book reviews are not traditional school assignments.

9   You can review more than one book at a time. Just group them by author, genre, subject, or series.

10 Book reviews are not book reports.

SO MANY BOOKS, SO LITTLE TIME

Every year, thousands of new books are published. But no one has time to read them all. That means we have to make choices. Choosing a book is a personal process as individual as each individual reader. We all have different tastes and tendencies. That's what makes choosing fun.

Enjoyable as it is, making the decision to pick one book over another is by no means a trivial matter. For one thing, there's a serious investment of time involved. The average novel might take the average reader eight to ten hours to finish. If we buy the book from a bookstore, we'll have to lay out a little cash, too. Readers want to spend their time and money wisely just like everyone else so they tend to take their book choosing seriously.

I'm one of those serious book choosers. If you ask me what I'm reading at any given moment, chances are good I'll have a title to report, sometimes more than one. I read almost every night before I go to bed and at other idle moments in my day. If I've got a break, I've probably got a book.

Deciding what I'm going to read next is a big deal for me. I hate making bad choices. So I think a bit before settling on something. I think about my mood and my current interests, of course. But I also pay attention to what other readers think about the books they've read. These people are book reviewers and I often find myself depending on them to help me make my decisions.

I love reading book reviews. On Sunday afternoons, my wife and I go down to the Orange County Social Club to visit with friends and to read *The New York Times*. What's my favorite section? The one devoted entirely to book reviews. I even have several books of book reviews at home in my library.

I love hearing what other people have to say about books. Reviews not only help me figure out the books I want to read next, they increase my understanding and enjoyment of books I've already read by allowing me to compare my thoughts with those of another reader.

Working with kids in school, I've come to realize that book reviews, along with the book talks that often precede them, provide some of the most enjoyable moments we have in class. Everyone seems to love talking about books and when that talk gets written down it seems to mean even more to us.

WRITING ABOUT WRITING

It may seem strange at first to write about something someone else has already written. But it's more natural than you think. Consider this: as you read a book, you have many different thoughts about it. If you're reading a story, most of those thoughts have to do with following the plot, thinking about the characters, wondering what's going to happen next, and so on. Why couldn't those thoughts be written down?

There's also another line of thinking you're probably involved in, though you might not be as conscious of it. This kind of thinking has to do with things like whether or not you're enjoying the quality of the writing, what your favorite part might be, or how the book compares to others you've read on the same subject, in the same genre, or by the same author. These thoughts are interesting, too, and are just as worthy of being recorded and shared.

Finally, I think we all have a responsibility to reach out to other readers whenever we can. It's true that reading is an individual pursuit. But that doesn't mean it has to be a lonely one. Around each book there exists a worldwide community of fellow readers. Whether they know each other or not, these people are bound together by a shared literary experience. Communicating with them through reviews enriches our reading lives and makes their experience of books better, too.

Miss Margot says

Unlike Mr. Peha, I don't read a lot of books. But when I do pick a book to read, it's almost always because I read something about it—a professional book review or even an e-mail from a friend. In fact, I chose the last book I read because two people e-mailed me that they thought I'd like it, and then I read a review in the paper. That's the power of book reviews.

A BASIC BOOK REVIEW

Even though each book review is as unique as the book being reviewed, most contain a small set of essential elements. Here's a good example of a basic review that sticks to the essentials.

A REAL EIGHT-YEAR-OLD GIRL'S LIFE

Touch of the flu? Egg in her hair? Poor Ramona!

Ramona Quimby, Age 8 is a nine chapter, one hundred and ninety page book about an eight-year-old girl in third grade. She started school with a surprise gift from her dad, only to have it stolen by a boy she called "Yard Ape." One day at lunch she tried to be cool and show off for her friends by cracking an egg on her head and found herself in a big mess. When flu season hit she learned how awful it felt to throw up in class. She and her sister learn about using good manners at the dinner table. As time goes by, Ramona and her family solve their problems, and learn to be more caring for each other. They also learn to be more considerate of each other when time alone is needed.

My favorite part was during a scene where Ramona's class is at lunch: "She took a firm hold on her egg, waited until everyone at her table was watching, and whack—she found herself with a hand full of crumbled shell and something cool and slimy running down her face." I thought that was funny because she wanted to be cool like the rest of her class, by breaking a hard-boiled egg on her head. But guess what, her mother was in such a hurry, she gave Ramona a raw egg. Whoops!

I think the most important thing the author wants me to know is that when my family may be having problems I can be of help by obeying them and not fussing, disturbing, and/or annoying them.

I liked this book because the author chose strong, powerful, descriptive words that made gross, imaginative pictures in my mind. Like in the lunch scene at school ("something cool and slimy running down her face") and at the dinner scene at home ("One edge of her meat was covered with tiny bumps.").

Ramona Quimby, Age 8 is one of the best Beverly Cleary books I've ever read because it pulled me in better than any other book in the Ramona series. (I have read six of her books.) It made wonderful pictures in my mind and sounded like a real eight-year-old girl's life. This made me want to keep on reading all the way to the end.

I recommend this book to good readers who enjoy good long lasting chapters (max 25 pages).

There are dozens of different things a writer can talk about in a book review. And though this reviewer explores only a few, she definitely takes care of the basics:

- **An original title.** It is possible to get away with titling a book review like this: "A Review of…[put the book title here]" but it isn't very entertaining and it isn't likely to draw readers in unless they've already read the book themselves or are considering it. It's much better to do what this writer did and come up with an original title. In this case, the writer has chosen to use a phrase that refers to why she liked the book so much.

- **An interesting lead.** Having a good lead is just as important in a book review as it is in any other piece of writing. I think this lead is clever. It's only ten words long and yet it gives us a sense that the book is about someone's life and all the things that happen to her.

- **A brief summary of the plot.** For readers who have not read the book, it's nice to offer a brief plot summary. A single paragraph, as the author has used here, is often all you need. Just don't spoil the ending. Readers hate that.

- **The reviewer's favorite part.** In a favorable review, one of the reviewer's jobs is to tell other readers why the book is worth reading. This is just one person's opinion, so we'd like to know as much about that one person's tastes as we can. One good way to discover this is when reviewers share the parts they like best.

- **The author's message.** Most stories you read will have a message, one important thing the writer wants you to know. This is what the book is all about—at least as far as the reviewer is concerned. The interesting thing about this is that different reviewers can read the same book and come up with completely different messages.

- **The quality of the writing.** In addition to talking about the story, we can also talk about the way it's written. Sometimes books have great plots but aren't well-written. On the other hand, I've read books where almost nothing happens at all, but the quality of the writing is so good I remain fascinated with it from cover to cover.

- **How the book compares with other books.** Sometimes, in addition to knowing if a book is any good, it's helpful to know how it is like or unlike other books in the same genre or by the same author. Even if we haven't read the book being reviewed, we might know one or more of the books the reviewer is using for comparison.

- **A recommendation.** In a way, the entire review is one big recommendation. But sometimes, right at the end, reviewers will say something more specific to define the kind of reader they feel will most appreciate the book.

Most book reviews can be broken down into different sections like I've done here with this one. In this case, the reviewer dealt with eight different things in her review: title, lead, summary, favorite part, message, writing quality, comparison with other books, and a recommendation. You can write many reviews with just these simple elements, or you can come up with others. For example, some reviews talk more about characters, while others talk more about plot, setting, language, and other important things.

TIP:

The great thing about writing book reviews is that you have a lot of freedom to focus on the things that interest you as the reviewer. The trick is to balance the review between things you care about and things that are useful to another reader who is trying to decide whether or not to read it.

THE THINGS THAT MATTER MOST

Relative to the books they describe, most book reviews are very short. In fact, I would suggest that most of yours run 500 words or less. The book you've read might be a hundred times longer than that (or maybe 400 times longer if it's the fifth Harry Potter book), so how do you say something meaningful and interesting about such a long book in such a short review?

The solution is to think carefully about the things that matter most to you as a reader.

Every book is filled with ups and downs. Even our favorite novel of all time has parts we find dull, difficult, or otherwise impossible to enjoy. While reading a good book, we run through a huge range of emotions. We also have a range of thoughts, many that go beyond the book itself to our own lives and the world around us. Your task in a book review is to bring to someone who hasn't read the book a sense of what mattered most to you as you read it.

A DIFFERENT KIND OF REVIEW

Because they come in all shapes and sizes, book reviews can be hard to categorize. Below you'll find a review that looks and feels a bit different from the one in the previous section.

In the review of *Ramona Quimby, Age 8,* the reviewer concentrated on presenting some of the basic elements of a review in a particular order. In the review below, young critic Micaela Arneson isn't thinking about essential elements or what order they're supposed to go in. Instead, she's thinking about what mattered most to her as she read the book and letting the review organize itself around each idea she comes up with.

A TALE OF THINGS BEYOND THE SURFACE

Hidden Talents, written by David Lubar, is about a boy named Martin who has a problem respecting authority and who has been kicked out of every single school his father has sent him to. His last chance is Edgewood, a school for the troubled. During the course of his stay, he befriends four unique boys, boys with strange powers. Together they must control their powers, with Martin as their coach, and save their school from being shut down.

Storybook to Reality

Hidden Talents has very strong characters. Martin is not your everyday troublemaker. Lubar creates an almost surreal aura around him, making his "problem" much more dramatic and intriguing. Martin's friends are also realistic outcasts: rejected, hopeless (to the world's eyes), and unique.

While the five friends battle their powers, they also battle other kids, specifically a group of violent, big, rude bullies. They are typical fictional bullies: strong, mean, and stupid. But Lubar adds his creative flare to make them less storybook and more real.

Hook, Line, and Sinker

The beginning of *Hidden Talents* is my favorite part of the story. Martin is looking out the window of the bus, staring at the barren landscape as the engine rumbles beneath him. No other kids are aboard, only the bus driver, a pot-bellied, muscle-bound man, bigger than three Martins put together. Gradually, Edgewood comes into view, its grimy walls looming overhead.

I think the beginning is the best part of the book because, unlike many other young readers' novels I have read, it intrigued me right away and kept me interested. David Lubar also answers most of the general questions we might have about Martin's life toward the beginning so the reader has important background.

At one point, Martin makes a somewhat nasty remark toward the bus driver and this adds a bit of humor. The way Edgewood looms in the distance increases the suspense. The reader knows that something big is up ahead but is left guessing as to what direction the story will take.

Beyond the Surface

It looked like Martin's life was over the minute he set foot in Edgewood. But over the course of the novel, he faces and battles his true enemy: himself. The novel ends as Martin returns home to battle the last thing that has bothered his conscience: his relationship with his father.

Hidden Benefit

Hidden Talents is a unique teen book. Most young adult books are exactly like one another, full of gossip and silly relationships; they often lack good plots and strong characters. But *Hidden Talents* tells an exciting and powerful story of an unwanted boy who, in the process of trying to find himself, grows as a person and helps those around him to find themselves, too.

In addition to being just plain fantastic, I think this novel could be very beneficial to teens who are struggling to find themselves or struggling to sort out family relationships.

There are many things to like about this review but the best thing to me is how much I feel as though I'm getting to know the reviewer in addition to the book she's talking about. I especially appreciated the following:

- **Caring about characters.** The first thing I noticed was how much the writer cared about the characters in the story. It wasn't just about the plot and everything that happened. The reviewer was looking for—and found—rich, complex characters she could relate to and identify with.

- **Looking below the surface.** Looking for deep characters usually leads readers to look for deeper meaning, too. I can tell, especially in the last two sections, that the reviewer is interested in looking below the surface of what happens to find aspects of the story that are truly meaningful.

- **High standards and serious intentions.** In the last section, the reviewer compares the book to other books written for kids her age. What she says about it makes me feel like the book is, indeed, as unusual as she claims. She's obviously a serious reader in search of serious reading.

- **Heading in the right direction.** I love the clever headings that introduce each section. This tells me that the reviewer is not only thinking of what's important to her, but she also wants her readers to have an enjoyable experience as they move through her review.

There's no one right way to write a book review. You can follow the same structure that the reviewer of *Ramona Quimby, Age 8* chose to follow. Or you can follow your heart like the reviewer of *Hidden Talents* did. All you have to do is tell your readers why the book is important to you—and entertain them a bit along the way.

BE A WRITER LIKE EL VEZ

El Vez has been called the world's most elegant Elvis Presley impersonator and "The Mexican Elvis." He writes songs, skits, and other stage productions. A talented musician and prolific recording artist, El Vez has recorded over twenty albums.

WHAT KIND OF WRITER ARE YOU?

I am a terrible writer. Lazy as heck. Wait to the last minute. I have bad punctuation and spelling and am very big on run-on sentences. I tend to use a collage effect in writing. Well, I do in my own mind—the piecing together of parts.

I write for my music. I write for plays or scenes. Bits for skit comedy. Long set-ups for small visual puns that usually I only understand. I write e-mails, too. I am a good e-mail buddy.

I'm a good re-writer. I like to take an existing piece and turn it into something else.

WHY DO YOU WRITE?

I write because I have to get something freed from my mind. Sometimes it's just banging around in there and the only release is to write it down. Alas, this ends up being on a scrap of paper. Once done to that extent, it leaves my mind and I usually forget about it. I get a big drawer of bits. This can work computer-wise, too. I have a big file of fragments. Maybe that's where the collage effect comes in. I try to string these little bits together.

Q

A

WHAT MADE YOU WANT TO BE A WRITER?

Necessity is what makes me write. Not really a love or a joy. Well, once in a great while it's a joy when it comes out clever. I didn't want to be a writer. Sometimes I write a song just so I can wear the outfit.

Q

A

WHAT ADVICE WOULD YOU GIVE TO A FELLOW WRITER WHO WAS JUST STARTING OUT?

Be organized. Write daily. Save everything, the good and the bad. Write even if it's bad. Don't be afraid to copy. It usually comes out different anyway. And if it doesn't, it's an homage. And then, if they figure it out they go back to the original source to see what your inspiration was and you have passed along that original inspiration.

REVIEW THE POSSIBILITIES

If you asked me to tell you the percentage of kids I work with who have written book reviews prior to working with me, I would sheepishly admit that it's very, very low. And yet, here I am spending an entire chapter on reviews and trying to make the case that I think you should be writing them all the time. What's up with that?

If you thought about it, I think you'd be amazed at the amount of reading you do. And if you thought a little more, you'd probably be just as amazed to discover how much thinking you do about what you read. I'll bet you even write a lot about what you read, though most of what you write is likely to be based on traditional school assignments. Perhaps you're closer to being a book reviewer than you think.

Still, if book reviews are not traditional school assignments, and if so few kids write them, why bother? Here are four reasonably good reasons:

- **Book reviews are fun.** I've been pleasantly surprised over the years about how much fun I have with kids when we write book reviews. I'll grant you that some of the fun comes from sharing our reviews in a group—something you can't enjoy as easily when you're writing at home—but there are plenty of ways to get this kind of interaction with other readers if you want it.

- **Book reviews are active.** Unless you're reading one of those super-large unabridged dictionaries and bench-pressing it between page turns, reading is a relatively passive experience. By contrast, book reviews are not. Book reviews encourage you to do something with what you've read. This makes you a better reader, a better thinker, and perhaps even a better human being—at least in my estimation.

- **Book reviews are real.** Most of the stuff teachers ask you to write about your reading simply doesn't exist in the world outside of school. I honestly have no idea where these assignments come from or what their value is. But I can tell you this: real human beings have been writing book reviews in one form or another for hundreds of years. Even when books no longer exist because we're all reading on computers, reviewers will continue to review them (they just won't be called "book" reviewers anymore).

- **Book reviews are cool.** Okay, we're not talking iPod cool here. But they are cool in a way. Here's the deal: a book review is your opportunity to render an opinion—good, bad or indifferent—on a work of art. This is your chance to have your say about somebody else's work and to influence others with your insights. It's a powerful position to be in. And power is definitely cool.

Assuming you now believe as I do that book reviews are worth writing, there are just a few other things I'd like you to know.

REVIEWS AT SCHOOL

I admit that writing reviews at school with your friends is more fun than writing them at home by yourself. Having a community of review writers—who are also readers, of course—provides a perfect audience for you to interact with. So one way to improve your book reviewing is to get your teacher at school to let you do it.

This is not as hard as it might seem. Most teachers would be so blown away with a student who actually wanted to write something about a book they might just let you write anything you want. I've noticed, too, that teachers who see kids writing book reviews, and get caught up in the wonderful discussions that accompany them, often want to do reviews on a regular basis.

TIP:

If you think reviews sound like fun, or at least like more fun than the assignments you're doing now, write a review and bring it into class. If your teacher says that he or she would prefer to have you write things called "literary analysis", "plot summary", "character sketch", or "compare and contrast essay", explain that you can do all of these in a much more interesting way through book reviews.

TALK FIRST, WRITE SECOND

Some of the best writing about books comes from talking about books. That's why I like to have book talks when I work with kids in school. Book talks can be formal or informal. In a formal talk, someone who has finished a book addresses the entire class, talking for a few minutes about the things that matter most, and then answering questions from the audience. In an informal talk, someone who isn't finished yet with a book might simply want to come up and share one interesting thing about what they had read that day.

Regardless of how long or how formal a book talk is, you'll figure out as soon as you do one that talking about your book helps you get ready to write about it. This is especially true when you get good questions from your audience. Knowing what your audience is interested in tells you a lot about how to write your review.

GENRE, AUTHOR, SUBJECT, AND SERIES REVIEWS

Though the typical review focuses on a single book, you don't have to limit yourself. As long as you can keep everything straight, you can review groups of books organized by genre, author, subject, series, or just about anything else that makes sense to you and your audience.

Technically, with more books to cover, there's more to do. But having more than one book gives you additional things to talk about. Comparing books is fun and easy. You also get to talk about why you grouped the books together.

REVIEWING NON-FICTION BOOKS

While the reviews I've shown you here have both been based on works of fiction, there's no reason you can't review non-fiction books, too. Reviewing biographies, autobiographies, and books about important events is virtually identical to reviewing novels. But reviewing informational writing can be a little different.

If you're reviewing a book about a certain kind of animal or about a specific subject like space exploration, for example, you may just want to share some of the interesting information you remember. You may also want to give your audience a sense of why the book is worth reading, even if they're not that interested in the subject.

If you're reviewing a book that tells you how to use a computer program, how to draw, or how to cheat the latest video game, it's important to realize that most people read these books to solve particular problems. Your most important task in this kind of review is to tell your audience how the book succeeds or fails in this regard.

IT'S NOT A BOOK REPORT!

Last but not least, there's one thing I want to be very clear about: a book review is not a book report. I don't know when book reports got started, but I wish they would stop. When I was in school, book reports involved answering a set of pre-defined questions a teacher had given us. It was more like filling out a form than trying to communicate something meaningful. I'm pretty sure our teachers assigned them simply to make us prove we were reading.

Writing book reports is not a good way to learn to love reading or to become a better reader. Book reports are a waste of time, energy, and imagination because they have no real purpose or legitimate audience.

A book report is a student being asked to prove to a teacher that he read a particular book by answering a list of questions that may or may not be very important to anyone. A book review is a real reader writing to other readers about real things for real reasons that really matter.

Miss Margot says

Since getting out of high school, nobody in the real world has ever asked me to write a book report. In my life as a professional writer, whenever someone wants me to write about something I've read, there's a legitimate purpose for it that has to do with the client, the project, or another part of my work. Book reviews can make writing about books in school more real. And they're certainly more interesting for teachers and other people to read than book reports. If your school or class has a paper, TV or radio show, or web site, start publishing reviews there. Or, if you can't get your school to do reviews, start your own book review blog!

Just Be a Writer

Author's Note

This is my favorite part of the book: the last part. As I mentioned way back when, I hate writing, but I love having written. And as soon as I wrap up this last little bit, I'm going to love having written even more. Except for one thing: I owe my publisher another book right away. Within mere hours of saving this document and sending it off to the production team, I'll be sitting at my computer once again with a blank Page 1 staring me in the face.

This is what it's like to be a writer.

Now, of course, there are breaks we get to take: a few minutes here and there to get a drink of water perhaps or a few hours of sleep between midnight and 6AM. I believe we're also allowed to take off three or four national holidays each year, but don't quote me on that because I lost my copy of the most recent union contract. Other than that, it's write, write, write—twenty-five hours a day, eight days a week, thirteen months a year until your fingers break off and your eyes fall out and you can't remember your own last name. Fifty, sixty years later, you get the gold watch and they wheel you off to the Old Writers' Home.

Actually, it's not like that at all. Most writers have a couple of working fingers and one good eye left when they retire.

The truth is, I have a lot of flexibility in how I spend my time and in the kinds of writing projects I take on. I don't have to write every minute of every day, and when I do, I have a lot of choice in the matter. Today, for example, I didn't spend much time at all on this book. (Don't tell my publisher!) Instead, I worked on an editorial I've been wanting to finish up. And this morning, even though I got up early and did a five-mile walk, I went right back to bed and slept in until 9:30AM!

Yes, the writing life is a very good life indeed. And here you are, right on the verge of living it yourself. After reading this amazing book, you have no doubt attained the skills and insight required to begin your life as a successful professional writer. As soon as you turn this final page, major publishers from every country on every continent will be calling to present you with lucrative contracts featuring fat advances and a generous share of the movie rights to your next idea. Your success as a world famous wordsmith is virtually guaranteed! Just pick up your phone and dial 1-555-BEAWRITER now to begin living the life you've always dreamed of.

Okay, so it's not that simple.

We started out together, eighty thousand words ago, talking about what it meant to be a writer. We looked at the writing process and a few important forms. We looked at some writing samples and went over several strategies. We talked about being this kind of writer and that kind of writer. We even looked at all those "Be a Writer Like Somebody So-and-So" things.

Now what?

Here's a secret: it doesn't matter. Don't worry about being a certain kind of writer. Just be the kind of writer you want to be. And if that's not any kind of writer all, don't worry about that either.

If you're like me, you'll go back and forth many times in your life trying to figure out whether or not you're a writer. And much as I would wish otherwise, neither this book nor any other book will do much to help you figure that out. The only way to figure it out is to write.

And you can start by writing to me, if you like.

If there's one thing every writer needs, it's other writers. Even though we all write alone, we shouldn't be lonely in our writing. We need to be part of a community of people like us, people who know what being a writer is like. Without other writers, it's hard to know if we're making progress. Without other writers, it's hard, too, to get help when things aren't going well and we feel like giving up.

So drop me a line. Let me know how you're doing. Ask me questions. Send me your latest piece. (Don't put me on your mailing list for the Joke of the Day, however. I hate those.) My e-mail address is *mrpeha@beawriter.US*. I can't promise to respond to every message I receive, but I do promise to read every message you send.

Thanks for taking all those hours to read clear through to the end. And if you just skipped here without reading anything else, thanks for at least taking fifteen seconds to do that. To be read is a writer's greatest reward. And even if all you read was this last paragraph, that's reward enough for me.

Goodbye. Good luck. And good writing!